CUNNY POEM VOL. 1

Published by Sorry House in 2017
First edition April 2014, Small Batch Books
Copyright Bunny Rogers
Copyright Sorry House LLC
ISBN: 978-0-9888394-5-8
Cover design by Erik Carter
Book design by Adam Robinson
For distribution or wholesale information
visit sorry.house
@sorryhouse

BUNNY ROGERS
CUNNY POEM VOL. 1

For Biff Brannon

Contents

"...You wish to be alone
Not studied
Nor put on display
Neopets are afraid of you..."

Shadow Usul by Link1429

My Art sucks

You know why
I dont have to tell you why
I'm sure
JUst like everybody else
I dont owe anybody anything!

Alison

no
nevermind
just dont say anything

Valentine's Day

I want a fine arts valentine
One that's steady and that's true
I want a fine arts valentine
I spend so much time in school
When I look around me
All I see is kids
Kids I'd like to spend the day with
Kids I'd like to eat a meal with
It's hard in school
to know your boundaries
it's hard outside
to know your boundaries
I'd like to touch some kids
I'd like some schoolkids
To touch me

Dark poem

Self-pity should be a crime punishable by death
Even Safety Has A Purpose
Goodbye Wednesday
Goodbye Dad
O, Columbine
O Water of Life,
Of Death

Cute

cunny4 lives indoors
drinking cartons of buttermilk
it makes her skin soft
it makes her nails hard

K

I'd fuck almost anyone
Seriously
But some are easier to love than others

Loving ru is easy

I think you are easy to love
I feel good when I am around you
I look forward to seeing you and
Am Accepting of your attention

Why

Wish I were Russian
So I could stop disappointing people
So I could have been in training
To be a Prima Ballerina
Or a Rhythmic gymnast
Or contortionist
By age 3

Why 2

In Russia
Graduating highschool is celebrated
With an event called
The Last Bell
Teen girls wear dark dresses
With lacey aprons
And large hair bows
I don't know what the boys do.
I bought a Soviet era schoolgirls uniform
from eBay
Size Youth Large
I can't wear it.
It doesn't fit me

Hiccup

Maybe church
Who am I kidding

3 years ago

Getting fat is easy
When you are beautiful
Whos to say
I don't have what it takes
Whos to say
I was wrong
talk to him about how u feel
maybe hes over u

my friend Catherine

told me how he loved me and all this other stuff
on how he wanted to die alone and other stuff

Untitled 1

trying to make you jelouse
i REALLY hope this helps because i CAN feel your pain

Untitled 2

Last week
I had the happiest day of my life
I don't know what tricked me into thinking
I was better
Or stronger
When I just had relatively less acne
I had the full attention
Of three male classmates
I was the center of the universe
I was at ease

God won't erase me

Prefer to wear dirty cute outfit
Than clean frump one
Okay and happens
Not a huggy type

Untitled 3

Fuck u
I love u
Fuck u tho
I love u tho

Andrea model

Andrea has porcelain skin
Andrea is not vegan
Andrea makes difficult work
Andrea writes a lot
Andrea does her homework
Andrea looks young
Andrea is sexually inexperienced
And unaware
Andrea has a fetish for constrictive fabrics
I am perceptive
Everyone is in love with Andrea
Three straight men in our grade
One shop tech
And a handful of L train commuters
Andrea needs love too
Andrea doesn't deserve to die
Want to start a fund to save Andrea

Dark Duck poem 2

Lost control of right eyebrow
Lefts okay
Have a Leif in school
Need help with my face
Need to relearn things and stuff
Need help

You don't love me yet

I'm embarrassed
And this would be okay
But this is what I know
So that's all there is
Later I will be sad about sex
Muffy stuff
Karolina Kosturova
I look pretty
Thank you God

Not my mama's feelings

If you want to kill someone
U hav every right to
Best wishes from my kitchen to yours

loyalties

Remember how confident I was about
How I would take care of myself.
I had plans in case you
went to jail, died, or left me.
I feel too heavy to be a butterfly.
What does a traditional heartbreak feel like?
My heart is a stone.
My heart is a sponge.
In my stone house
I see the importance in reading books.
Wholesomeness is insulting and
I am scared to think your word is not law.
My body doesn't matter to heaven but it matters.
I want to sleep in my office,
by my rocks.
I want to sleep through centuries.
Elliott Smith is dead and
Anyone who has ever been in love with an addict
understands this song.

my dowry

What kind of dog is that? I smile
i hope he feels comfort from my big blue eyes
animal compansions
Ack know it is crucial time
feel your absence very strong
what do you know?
i got one
i got a dog

But bunny never came

Harry not again the TV.
Careful is different than
Cold and reserved and suspicious.
You have to be so careful.
Go home cop daddy....
It will be quiet soon...

"Every living creature on this earth dies alone."

Michael Scofield would stop at nothing.
You are looking at two folded cranes.
You are looking at two painted turtles.
I hope you enjoyed them.
You are looking at two painted turtles
and the occasional crane.

There are
Two sets of footprints in the sand
Charting your life's path, and
During the hardest times in your life
You see only a single set of footprints.
You ask Agent Mahone,
Agent Mahone why when I needed you most
Did you abandon me
And Agent Mahone says
That that was when he carried you.

Kate and Sawyer

The case of Kate and Sawyer—
Two runaways with fallen down hearts.
(Don't worry they come back.)
Never trust Kate.
Never trust Sawyer.
You never know for how long
Love will lay dormant.
Tree Swallows, Wrens, and the Sparrow
run away when you close to the nest.
Tree Swallows are another story.

Safety hurts

I like to see you in your room.
I spent all my time in the basement.
I like seeing you.
You never sat in the chair.
you never forgot I hate it.
I never want to break any rule or law.
Safety hurts,
in bed where I belong.

My apologies accepted

It gives me great pleasure to see you safe.
Feeling safe is most important.
I love red...
Because I am dramatic.

Army and Risotto

I dont feel bad for wanting to fuck my cousin
because that is very common
I am pretty sure.
either way it seems like delicate information
so I don't talk about it.
I would have done well with a brother.
I only want one brother and one dad.
That's how it should be.
but right now I have two dads,
and at least two brothers.
My sisters definitely arent my sisters
and Brigid wont have me.

July 18 2012

Voice mailbox breakdown (14):
Dad (8)
Filip (3)
Ben (1)
Grandpa Pedersen (1)
Shawn (1)

Doomed to be a "vodka girl"

i would not want to go to the airport right now
now u know how my dad feels
it was my ankle, and it's O.K.

Poem for Bernadette

i am very forgiving, watch this
U are looking at a very forgivable very beautiful
  heartbreaker
i look at you and i have no idea who you are
i forget your name all the time
you can laugh safely because this is what i wanted
Its all tailoring u know that

Giada at home fade to white

I can tell wen ur home
I know wen ur home
u didnt make me do anything

Birthday poem

It means so much to have your words remembered
It means so much to have your pain acknowledged
People use proper spelling and grammar when they want
  to return the hurt.
Sex is disgusting because I am disgusting

My old issues with hugging.

hugs are an excuse to touch the body of someone
You cant for whatever reason go to bed with.
This is very typical Capricorn.

Two poems for my parents

INTJ powerhouse

Scared my dad is going to die
wish I could stop thinking about evolution
I dont want to explore my options
I like boring

I would look beautiful in any one of these dresses

I was so hated
I felt my mother's embarrassment and confusion
You have to L'express yourself but
Presents should not come from a place of pain

Trees grow up (requiem)

it isnt that big of a deal
i want to come home, too
Harold wait
Dear, sweet Harold
i will never wear sunglasses

Lisas theme (Bunny hot and cold)

Like u im psychic but smarter
unlike smart people I like working easiest to harder
but i knew the whole time
thats why i went crazy

I dont look down cuz I dont want to know

Here is a pair of armwarmers to keep your arms warm
here is a box of Shawns shoes
here are five of Shawns sweaters
This is a tour of my house and these are my things

Dinotopia (Nessie's theme)

What's got you blue, Betts?
jealous warters have me scared of the ocean.
when Jared Leto tells Jennifer Connelly's character,
There is never music playing.
She says that she really hears it
That she believes him

I Love You!

You are excited to show me things!
I believe you when you smile!
You have An interest in my interests!
Your arms wrap around me twice!

For me twas horror

Breaking news i dont love anything
so tired and all this.
it feels necessary to drink in the beginning
its like really okay
and we talked about it
and it like doesnt matter

Trace amounts of cp

I was scared but I overcame
deep respect for my addiction
thank you for touching me.

Selfish

when u confirm something as being hilarious
laughing is infections
u just "fall into it"

Society

i do it all, fuck you!
egomaniacs dont kill themselves
im going international
im going to die in long island

Less Stones

people adjust it doesnt matter.
it takes a long time to name something.
company takes time
Sometimes, people are crazy
it wasn't about me

Analysis u can trust

question what u know and what u know I won't say
This is good indicator u can handle me
When u think about it trust doesn't matter at all
Matters about as much as
Only kindness

Genetique (schizo)

I know u are smart
U treat people in a very smart way
its amazing how people change their tune
its amazing when people change their tune

We are 30 (You don't know the pain it feels)

You're hurting him!!!!!!!!!!!
His sufferings were real!!!
His tears were real!!!!
(He looked back at me and he scared me.
he had, we had eyes full of tears
he promised to write me back but when??? When we are 40?)

Scylla

oh my god
as if you are first person to decide I am beautiful
don't you understand I am in control here
What's the last thing you put out of its goddamn misery
INFP or not my sufferings were real
Giving up is fair
Giving up is beyond fair

Rat friend (for Ben)

gimme context
build up my ego
word never gets back to me
youre like my only point of entry

The company will protect you...

I will smell different if i cut my hair
after a certain point long hair becomes rebellious
at the same time I have to laugh because
how can they let that happen
and on top of that people just shouldnt do that

company

We begin building a strong, long-lasting friendship
with a foundation of forgiveness
It is nice seeing you enjoy yourself
You have great energy and emit positivity
This draws people near to you
I would like to let you keep me company
You will never harm me
I appreciate your time, energy and money
I appreciate you reaching out
It lets me know that you are interested
That you have little to no difficulty
Keeping self-motivated

dotyk

It is important to keep my cellophone charged
I have to provide the tools by which to reach me
they have reason to touch you
I need to keep doors "open"
Weirdos get killed that's why

What if someone told u you were significant?

I like u when youre coherent
Well...........
Does it work like that? It doesn't work like that

Once I had a morning too
(grizabella's theme)

dont u dare claim me
i will make u proud
u wolf
u predator
u beast
i'm so used to u somehow

Sissy

shes small
she smells
she misses you

Blood will spill blood

Twin Peaks was created to tell Harold's story.
Twin Peaks had nothing to do with Laura
it had everything to do with Harold.
It's about Harold and it was always about Harold.

The coldest shoulder

Two childhood animal friends
find themselves forced to become enemies.
No one breaks up with you
Everyone just goes away

Ideas aren't the issue

In the end it doesnt even matter
because practicality is key
A trapped insect is your responsibility to save
dont blow it

What happens to me

I am so animated and full of life wow
I am so afraid of everything wow
Its not unusual to be scared of everyone
I DONT WANNA TALK ABOUT IT WOW
I DONT WANNA TALK ABOUT IT

tasti (For Shawn)

Trust peanut butter to conceal you
an opportunity to better myself?
no thanks
everybody looks great

I can't wait to share you

All men are cops
cuff me Im guilty
cuff me Im guilty
cuff me Im guilty

Pectus excavatum

Hi Bunny its Dad
Are you ok I heard you vomiting
To be objectively beautiful you need to be a vessel
It were an objectively cold house I kept

@ one with the screaming in my head

Adorability is fuckability
because children are adorable
and men want to fuck children
Acknowledge or die wow
You are dead to me

Almost love

u cant expect people to keep quiet but i wish you could
consideration went into this dont ignore
God I miss Donna

Rip VoDKa

go easy on urself
dont be so hard
nobodys worth it
nobody cares

soft flameless candle
(Midian City dregging)

Here they are, reflected
Deranged like cold interiors
Im kissing you right now

Sympathy is pity

Imagin me in 10 Years wow scary

g

im unique~
think for myself~
borderline alcoholic~

Marion

him is my favorite word
Little boy soft flameless candle
left our siblings lonely
i never saw it coming................

insipide, tout comme moi
(tasteless, just like me)

I skipt piano again............
do u worry i will start to feel different?
It hasn't felt wrong enough to stop
You deserve everything and
Its not my body anyhow.
Stay in bed wait for me

filip was like "im never doing that again"

you don't have to be convinced of the past
if you choose not to and take necessary steps to quiet it

How 2 convince urself of what has been established

He is allowed to look at me like that because
Things happened and Something was established
But he looks so dumb and creepy I feel nothing
When he looks at me like that it means
Things happened and something was established

Swan pussy

Everybodys vibrating
And you know what else
Everybodys got a tail
So don't feel too bad

Master Manipulator Theodore Bagwell

Leave Me Out of It
say my name again
deem me recruitable

Every rose

I want big things to make you think of me
Like rain
And chase bank

martyr

I was built to be the exception
Look at me
Look at me of course im excited
with so little effort
with such conviction

In disgrace not much wrong

my aching knees right where you left me
If u cry when u think about how u treat people
Ur doing something right

Happy Fathers Day you know who you are

u have to laugh in the morning
I mean me, a steak dinner
you could spend lifetimes adjusting to rot stink
weird to go outside and see other people still alive
still going outside
But can still provide impressive company
for all the dads out there

legal pad (ought not)

me? A prisoner inside my own body?
Impossible
Hark, more evidence of my psychic abilities
A place of true emo where nothing is fun
I would have liked to move closer
to a lesser amount of characters
but alas

lamentations

i wouldnt do it if i didnt want to
sike!
If youre not first youre last
Timbre!

the science of self distribution

no regrets
not ever
not in this body

cp direct (sociopath)

that was a dangerous thing i said
sometimes, sometimes there wont be a way back
you cant watch your train pull away from the station
with u on it
how thoughtful
how u intend to operate

beware of girl art

Lo, I am with u always
Hark! my type

cloak

your name is so soft
your heart is so soft
your hug is so warm
your eyes are so kind
your grip is so light
your touch is so light
your eyes are so scared
your kiss is so scared

Chimneypiece

its not about ease its not about comfort
Keep thinking about your cock
We all has attachment issues
Still with you still kissing you

still holding

you are a crane, you are a paper crane,
floating through the sewer system of
a maximum security prison

Melting Michael

Here I am, kissing you
Falling asleep on my shoulders
married under Marble Collegiate church
my only real skate

Deer deer

Bessie's ethics
Bessie's fucked ethics
wearing that stupid man suit
Lisa's bright
Lisa's dark
defining my windows

deeply bugged

Is it visible?
It mustn't be
someone would say something
someone would help
Can u say that thing about audience again
but then how does everyone know
Can u say that thing about audience again

Tweener (triple d)

Its still so intimate still
Months and months after pet loss.
after everyones been dead for a while
Even after the new cat replaced the old cat.
sharing random acts of violence personally
sweet tears falling watching food network
wishing I cared about your sense of closure
I am still anxious

Old bones

Toddler brigids face grows white
even her eyelashes
Our red walk in closet
That really bad movie

bold Comp ex

Never make excuses bc theres never enough material.
You will always accuse the ones you love
everything is equally embarrassing
u are the hot beating center of humanitys humiliation

cassandra

Stil hang on wrong side of tracks
You are an asshole and it is okay
Adjust the cause is out of the question
Sincere thanks got us into this mess
got us here in the first place

Marcs summer

Active and actually very simple
That's what it was like
I cant say no so don't ask me

Getting buried w my dog sanity

Want my legs eaten by lava
trick cars into hitting me like a dog
drown in tub
steamrolled

can't promise anything

Its just a bed
you have to understand what kind of pressure
this puts me under

Michael the impossible snowflake

Saint Tancredi at my shoulder
When im slumped in the shower or an alley
im laying down in a bath tub
trying to make my days as short as possible
is everybody special
special never used to be a question

our compr♡mise

Trying not to roll down my window too far
needing u really
Counting crows smell of hotels
I am bleeding

Lincoln lust

what else is there to care about when you don't
get carded anymore
when u can do whatever u want
what people consider important- defragging, debugging
what people consider important- diamonds
wearing black at my wedding
Dont push me im "doing my best"

Lyrically sound (window seat)

Giv him something u need. in order

Hope it comes ok

they were nothing ok fine they were nothing
help me if i get another word out
help me if i get a word in edgewise
everyone got it the first time

Psychic tears

Regardless. whatever you do just stop saying for sure
cuz you never know
When he will leave why he will stay
and u dont feel anything
Hard to make progress when everyone that loves u
is a junkie
Can u tell, make sure of it

Avoid agnes

Our shared armrest. the one that folds up
Hey, do u understand me? x10
Sad clown girl is too pretty a descriptor
Worthless with sad face
ill be home for dinner

Thankfully common (feels close)

What's great about it is light, good touch feel
What's not so great is vulnerable

Heavy deepest lisp

Interested in world of fiction
And all interesting stories

Why we never took her serious

theres no difference between me and her
as i look at her crows feet
We are the same our appeal is the same
as i notice the seat to my right is empty during rush hour
As puddle of mudd comes clean

Morgentown

Regressus ad infinitum
chocolate brown Hydrangem
black roses, blue roses
black and white roses
Halloween roses

pedophile

i will always defend you
i want to tell everybody else just stop
you will always be in the right
you are pure

For all the wrong reasons

I miss you too
Its raining
I could have sworn I handled it
Then all of a sudden I hate cats

dad

ceramic black butterflies
ceramic blue herons
ceramic grey swans

the symbol of the face always turned away

We wil die in this life and life wil say gbye
we will all say goodbye in this life

prety ok

if u care about one thing u have to care about everything.
how much i like the name cath
with a more complete understanding of Alvin

misrepresented invisible conversation

i dont feel what u feel
its a gift and a curse

pillhead

Fair is fare we all share the ride so we all pay for the ride
if he makes the exception for me
he would have to make it for everyone

teaers

theyre just nervous tears
displaced tears
am i a good actress or the worst actress?
I can talk about it now
I know I can talk about it
Its just hard

the living novel

we have a history
I die knowing good

Beast ultimate

All I have is art and toxicity
People h8 change
Me2

Well this broken girl is signing off

last thing we need is time lapse of blonde child
becoming adult
female 20 something struggling with doll aesthetic

shades of berny

berry
burgundy
merlot
cabernet
maroon
cranberry
plum

telepathy

people are not like us.
people forcibly frustratedly shape ur hands
if its more depressed than u want it to be
chair shows depression more than u like it to be
I am not afraid to force you out of my chair.
I will make it very clear
My relationship with my chair

no chair no pain

every chair a ghost
every day a hope
every day a heartache

squirtle

going to rain for a week
lonely and slow
blue ice hearts melt in the bathtub
fingers tapp into what u were once

different points in manhattan

Adjust cause if i have to be like them
Adjust position from different places in the wall.
Adjust the cause to make it ur own

mandalas de masones

hard enough to say it once
Janet please,
Janet this

Early records

eating clay and the like
a game about pleasing everyone can u address this?
happy steven likes me

even allen in defense and validation

collecting infp butterflies
and crushing them
Lovingly, detatchetly
is anything as cold?
special recognizes special
hurt recognizes hurt

Weight is finally back to normal

my window fell out
and killed a really nice plant
my very first watering plant
Five petals build a human face
squeezing until I cant see it

As if wat is perceived as strenth

The voices in my head say youre crazy
I laugh at you because you are all the same
Take my American girl doll Sabbath set
Take my dignity
you and your fat cat vocab
Feed me mud and light everything on fire
United in death ill see u in hell

Always crashing the same car

You just...make a filter!
U Conquer processing
U move on
There are beaches in Memphis!
There is careful implication
There are seconds of attraction and hidden heat
That's it!
Alertness is your most attractive quality
Dgaf about ur beliefs
Shopping happy
sleeping happy
drinking happy
You crash the same car
you trade the old girl in again

0:-|

i am a vegetable

comedys pretzel tradegys pumpkin

root vegetables are strong and stubborn,
like all farm animals.
Did you know: Pumpkin is a fruit?
Pumpkins are fruits in mourning, like all squash.
mushing down with their curly green pig tails.
Pumpkins are read slow, like all sad things.
Like pumpkins people rot from the inside out.

Rich history of some bad people

I cant believe the titanic sank
Agonizing efforts to legitimize this look and feel
undoubted regret trying to crack this cookie

Easy math

angel faced and ever hesitant
i wouldnt call it a bag of trix
but i would call it a bag of advantages
in every cinderella story there is the dark story,
there is the shadows
cant decide if you would rather fuck an angel or a child
I am hiding because I am not always interested
in having my patience rewarded

Otherless walls

Let him put it this way
Most things look like a frowning face
when michael died he took a piece of me with him
Still, here we are
Only holding onto u for safekeeping
u in your earplugs

Structured hat

I feel cool in this hat
Days without structure fall apart
Very responsive to authority
Understand paternal direction
Understand and welcome

Depression hurts everyone

Floating from house to house to house
If not a teacher dad then who?
if you are loved is a comfort
Admonishing would be a kind word
You would smile wen i smoke

Sorry (everyone)

So ur saying...im different
Yes, I will take it
R u fucking stupid
Of course I will take
Chosen
Special
Exception
My life is one really long precious moment
precious moments all throughout my birth month
like tiny garnets
None of which I registered
The living novel is heavy and empty and somewhere else
How can you stay aware if you cant remember?
Btw Ur subjective assessment confirms nothing
I am nothing

As ur soul gives up

precious moment
precious memory
precious musical

sexually appaeling

true story
sad story
my story

exit house Sobieski sob story

Purple curtains part and im crying a river
That leads to your bedroom
I am jealous and it makes me ugly
I am ugly inside and if it is not yet obvious
it is only a matter of time before it overtakes the exterior
Because I deserve it
How do u rid yourself of evil because I am miserable
Obviously u have a better grasp on things
On managing hatred
You will be okay
You are good, you started good
There are people that will always be good
And people that will always be bad
There are good people that go bad
but they go back and forth
Because it's fun, and they are good
They deserve to have fun
Regardless, they will make it to heaven
There are bad people that go good
But that's a very black and white commitment
and I'm happy for them but it's not for me
Me I am bad
And this is how it is

Resistance and yes corruption
This is wat destroys beauty
Its not always something
On or off, All we know is theres a wagon

poin is pain

i miss that day
i miss that day in histroy

pumpkin falling apart at the seams

im in a pit roast
im on the menu

Der Unhold the ogre

I Can't stop thinking of dying?
Truly unlimited reverie all alone
Flood angels, mud angels, blood angels
A prison study

signature moment

stuff just kept coming out stuff just kept pouring out

depressed and innocent

Why
Did you send that anne of gg .wav at me
What's on today's roster
Me,
looking at my butt, in accordance w the scriptures
envisioning my future
As an unloved pig marm

Pip the universal collaborator, teacher figure

Teach me to be strong when the characteristics
Of my victim belong to a group I hate
Neverending teardrops but no sympathy
Im gross im so gross
Curb-destined in the company
of smashing neighborhood pumpkins
U lay here
Ur worst nightmare came true
Paralyzed in view of my face

r.i.p. michael s.

Im just so happy look
I don't wnt to hurt people
But I hav to
Michael rest in piece
Every nosebleed I hav ill think of u
I don't want to hurt people anymore
But I have,I do,I will
I hav to
Michael rest in piece
Every nosebleed I hav ill think of u

Same fuckin kid

Still same dumb fuckin kid
w drug ravaged 80 year old body
Fuckin birth defects
fuckin face

Train hottie

Long faced like my mother
As great a man as I a shitty fuckin woman
A young John Abruzzi
A real weasel

Ode to Ina Garten

how easy was that?
How fun does that look?
How fast was that?
How good does that look?
How bad does that sound?
How bad can that be?

damasol

Disbelief that im stil alive even tho
we get it we got it this is hell n im exactly where im supposed
Fifty shades of grey clown
Everyday feels like forever

Because who could ever learn to love a beast?

assuming u correct this on ur own
assuming u achieve the impossible

Snowflake

behind the impossible
in a dark surpise
an only angel

love is afist in the air

when u push me
my heart bleeds for all these young ppl
when u punish me
u make me wanna do something worth the punishment

club die

You are so grounded
Married and Sober
Now you cant say 23 & confused
Or can u...?

cite men

Life is a pretty strong word
Are u sure that u mean it?
take a guess-
It's something between wat feels best and wats killing him
It hasn't been an option for years now
It looks like a cloud

**You know your place in the sky,
He knows his way in the dark**

Im an artist
Im an angel
Kill for me
Die for me

Have the sens have the decency

You cant escape delusion but u can make commitment bulletproof
Ice be my shield
you're all I have and more baby
I cant hold my own so u say im amazing baby
ive never seen my body in porn
ive never seen my body in anything

unusuble chaire

unusual chair
sits in the corner
between two walls
someone sits on her
someone close to her

Vail's first snow

Big secret snowflake
With parasitic tendencies
i dont want these feelings
across a canyon
a snowful wail
unfolds a snowing mystery

All the men who love me!

Common complaint is apologies are hollow
Wake up and put my head through a wall

Strange chair Samantha

Love is strange
It takes a rare breed of monster to meet
the challenge of accommodation
Sick fucking weirdo freak
Samantha said she wanted to know
what it's like to kill someone
How will her bloodlust end??????

Men who actually think about me

show me a pic of me that looks like me
so i "know"
"so i know"
for future "reference"
"for future reference"

Angels to ashes

Harlequin angel
Stowaway angel
a step of light
a step of shadow

i know u can see me i thought

I know you would never hurt me intentionally
I know because its me. Im the one who said it.
you trust me in a way.
Imagine that
Your lies as truths

Operative love conditional love

i promise to love.
though as I write this, raindrops are falling
Things arent perfect so
I promise to love in sickness
Make whatever advancements
Pull whichever strings
Like I always say
Does it make sense or is it confusing?
Its ur call
Like I always say Im too smart for this

Poisonous snow

Everyone has stupid men in our lives
that are sweet
My heart is in the wrong place
Sufficient example of toxic intelligence
Emotional intelligence is another way of indicating
wilting entertainment
With art feelings are clear
I stand by the manipulation
With people feelings are muddy
I want to be a good person
You made michael significant
How do i put this lightly

A pile of scraps

You can kill the beast
in no way is it in danger of going extinct
You will not get the doll in this case
you cannot kill the Beauties
You can kill the beast
You wrapped both wings and you shut your eyes
She would not have run away
if you had not frightened her
You can kill the beast
You have to break each door open

u cant squueezw blood from a shoe

u cant squeeze blood from a stone
other times i will resentment for the same reasons
then again my drug/alcohol use is on the upswing
you cant draw blood from a shoe
or anything that pulls back or spills blood
i dont want a man that can be mean
or find me at the cause of his anger

shadow smile

Open palms
A thousand nights
Blood sweat and tears pottery
My Lord smiles stumbling into happiness

I cant tell with men

The only people that die are ready to die
They take u home to mechanically cut you
They have trouble cumming even when they rape you
They come on slowly like strangers

dead rose anticomedy

Once the roses had withered and died
The stalker
took the ribbon her dad gave her and replaced it with his
Opened a new relationship
Walked outside and convincingly owned everything he touched

black comedy

I have to leave the house
At a loss
permanent loss of pigmentation
sensitive to sunlight
drug addict
alone

Clown by association

I used to smile to say hello
shaking your hands wildly
echoing tree stump names
I'm married
I have kids
You'd be surprised
A book in my guilt and honor
embroidered titling
glass companion

Maybe i wont get raped anymore

Guilt is doing what you want
We would have found each other sometime,
somewhere along the line, anyway
Guilt is doing what you wanted
In the end you marry your illness

pretty marry

elliott future
elliott failure
elliott fair

Welcome to the stupidest movie
none of your pain is real

Buddy convinced was fucking u was never fucking u
Never really fucking u at all
When doors open in courage humiliation
Distribute ur guilt by talking nonstop

pitseleh

she is asking you to see her pugalo
And she smells good and she feels healthy

Sister h

Its Melt down month
Crying out rocks and minerals
Rocks and minerals
my tree, my girl, my room
I had to look away sometimes
I had to look away

Getting Ready For Bed

I wake up and its Monday
I go to sleep and its Tuesday
A kiss goodnight can be a kiss goodbye
Its Tuesday and I want to die

Do this in remembrance of me

Remember this crushing day and the weight
of your stupidity.
NO one is exempt there are NO options
and there are NO alternatives.
Welcome to the stupidest movie...
None of your pain is real.

DarklyDeceived

I look up to spell remembrance
I find alternatives for "excitement" and other nails in coffin
u stop being the picture
u start being the frame
You have stopped being the picture
You have become the frame
steps to recoil escape this room, play
Overly eager for u to learn my name, Leave me alone

A hesitant yes and sweet consequence

Forced incest to intensify this pain
For those closest to core of this pain
A stone for Unica Zürn and still happy, blind
Make it harder for me to get out of bed

Porcelain workshop

my teeth are like falling out from pukinng so much
sometimes i find him really sexy and hot,
other times i think he is ugly and clumsy
and he reminds me too much of myself.
i think my teeth are falling out too

The sensitive comic

I know I've got a guilty face
I want to sit in a cell and turn my back away from you

Tears on the rock

Some things probably get left behind
with my knees curled into my chest
"You've got to kiss and hug—
Words aren't enough" I think
as I tear it into pieces now
Can one innocent child bring this family back together?
Or is it too late?

Black skeletons sitting at the dinner table

unusable house
unusual chairs
twisted family
lost ghosts

Princess Dirty Bun Emergency Bunvival guide

Your age doesn't really matter to this point.
Black pudding is pig blood.
Look im sick of u perverted men falling in love with me.
and expecting mountains in return.
u bore me.
if u arent a drug dealer u are useless and therefore repulsive.
I close my eyes and think back to Grandma ROgers
brook and raspberries.
I dip my feet in the cold water.
very out of character, I know
SKipping.
chirping.
drug hunting

piggish

Howd u become? high energy loving puzzled sock

hmmm Maybe there is a beast...hmmmmm

hiscomment and i die

poim for texas

i miss nothing about u
u ruined my life

another 30min n ud be in the clear but

At the end of the movie little claire danes looks toward
mario batali to cope w dysfunction of family life climax
This resonates much like maggie gyllenhaal in sherry baby
singing to dinner table of dead ppl
fighting in halfway house
i see lanky drug dealers on the corners
an my want is palpable
but imagine a long term relationship
and know it would see same fate as anything else
creeping disgust
gradual abandonment
for the first time I want to be given another chance
to start over
this is wat i want when i see high schools
in small towns
or rural aereas
skilled in dismissing regret but how to hide my shame
in isolation like this
just like little claire danes
except little claire danes is played by Sarah Bolger

For the cloudy-hearted

Follow ur heart when u can
Fold when u cant
Tuck ur do gooder lovers in a rocky pocket
Endure

I deserve a chance honey

Brains can be a challenge
Berry your weakness
Mutilate the earth

Precious moments are forever

I can wipe that smirk off my face this instance
Authority I thought was pretend authority is real authority
This is not prison
I am Arrogant
This is not prison

amanda

As a determined creature
you sound more poetic
I feel very old and I want my partner to physically reflect this
I love life
I just hate mine

daniel/denial

Type ur softest
A cat clue is a gift because its false and comforting
like a heaven for pets
Like a netted whale. like ur girlhood pal..
u kissed and cared about and included
in ur one person cat club
recommended for dead and/or adorable
the summer is sticky and u wait 16 Years
n the bugs dont come
The summer is 16 Years longer
Wat about the feelings i have inside
do i just pretend?

Love of my life

I slept on the left side of the bed
ignoring the male mosquitos on the wall
and accusations from friends
I held tight to Radio's little body
All your friends have gone and we miss you
they miss radio and his little boy
Male mosquitos are completely harmless
and target oranges
I slept on the left side of the bed
ignoring the guilty as charged and just as stupid
I squinted my eyes and decided to exhale

"visitors"

I had a dream I was your hero with mangled hands
I woke up with a UTI
We share health issues that make it hard to walk
hes got health issues im not sure totally
he looks like a druggie
he has friends though
people like lungs

together together

Together problems of the past assort themselves by color
Dad's gift becomes as wide and empty as dad's lake
and we find ourselves engulfed again
I can't count on nothing
I blanket personal shames in symbolic family tragedies
I receive visitors like I'm terminal
"Problems of my past"
or my words should have never been said
Demons cast underground restart and say hi again

A true mute is too tempting

Broken people don't get warm and won't get whole again
I don't want to touch my body anymore (anywhere)
and yeah, I have fallen leaves
waiting on thin ice
It's more important for you to be there
You're already something (special too)

untapped cunntential

for my birthday a lot of money
for my friend a lot of money
for u anything
a photo of me
a song
ulcers

royalty

u r purple like a bruise
u are wet like a mop and a pussy
u are my confidant
u are unfortunately all i have
u are a dehydrated pea i slamdunked jumping
on a stack of twin beds

**the only way ucan enjoy
revenge is if u r insane**

at the end of the book of ur life u will flip back to the first
page not frantically but calmly and u will repeat aloud but
mumbled "i must b in here...somewhere..."

Miss Bunny Havisham

Feeling safe is...
haggis
agnes
And i have a problem...
My beautiful black eye
they KEEP LYING until im in the trunk of their car

Lakebottom wood

i dont want 2 breed more things that norbordy needs
Sad old newspaper and crumpled in knots
He came in the room in the middle of the night
and he startled me
when did i shut down?
and he look me in the eyes with this invitation
i never held clues for you

A broken goat drowning a broken goat

watch the repairshop patrons escape priorities
I fumble with needles and bind beads together
Another sample for support facilities so strictly business
I refuse the magnifying glass and continue to hate them
"Looking for something to lighten up a dark corner?"
Company at the foot of your bed to garble your griefings
More eyerolls from me and I stay behind the counter
knowing how fine im not
I place my palms flat on the work bench because
the whole surface is moving

All the wood is wet

Wooden lips
Wooden hug
stale hug from a scarecrow
Don't promise what is outside
What God would make

zsmiserable hateful

Dear sister with brown jacket and brown teeth
i offered the hands I thought were wax for a reason
i hoped to write professionally
i sat you down in book signings
i watched my head snap to center
i slid down the drawbridge
i faced the edge to disappear
Please angel, accept this help
practice a belief in improvement
middle children are not only children
may u suspend our differences
win for mom and dad

treatment or deaf

Theres seemingly more than we can pronounce
and I fear the voices dampening
Imagin u were a social smoker
Archiving the habit
You gotta txt file with your sk8
and you gotta txt file with your real skate
The paranoia never left it
just chewed its way thru bed socks and boarded windows

black wolf designs

from an early age luxury affords me then her soul
if you chopped off my legs they would grow back longer
O grant us the pleasure of your shitty prescence
A sofa overhaul into new lvls
A remote station on a blistering sun
Demote Tara, Karen, Alvita
Pick up work next Tuesday!
Keep it
Custom, Custom, Custom

i cant imagine a life without drugs

In the future, when everyone finds out
I am no darling dolly
but a fraying velcro door fixture
A great costume for halloween
Attachable bow at tail, perforated leggings, mini hat
and a quarter mask
She might be broken but she is still sweet,
Distribute her weight well:
Cry my river, or brooke, or fucking dribble, Salinger
Entertainment depends on violence and my pain is
at the heart of your violence
However slow, and weak.
The middle of October and so he stirs, turns,
suffocates in his sheets
and falls into recovery.
Ashamed, I pick the novelty stockings away
from the greying floorboards, your closet.
I pull them over those grotesque and spiky mountains
Dotted, slobbered knees.
Me, your button
a Darling pull-doll.
Me repeats the names of women you've ribbon-up
and dotted with pet names

in my spherical walnut cavity and the closest
I will encounter to a treasure chest or anything special.
Grigory was never here and neither were I
in this Cry me a river, Salinger
in this Devon Aoki illustration.

snowflake sand (snow)

The middle of october feels like a Wednesday.
brick by brick i make a breakfast plan.
i stay inside for 72 hours and when i stand in the backyard
i want to inhale the fresh air between puffs of cigarette smoke,
and appreciate it as something alive but field trips last five
minutes long.
I develop large arms.
I never enter the bed and cry in the mornings or on the train
sometimes.
I imagine a cat named ketchup,
or myself as the shell of a cat and disgraceful,
messing up the sheets all by myself or peeing.
there are saints among us that are too drugged to participate
but i am inside with my square ass and fat arms.
So where will no get you?
No help that is all you.
Slim arms.
Make your arms more slim.
this winter is not cold but more beautiful.

Untitled new

you dont love me anymore
you dont have to keep pretending
you seemed disgusted by my appearance,
as you always do when im fucked up
you do not like the person i am
you have good friends that care about you
you have a family that loves you dearly
your presence made me feel disgusting and wrong, as a person
my presents were an attempt to show you that i still love you
i have been absent
i have been absent for everyone
i wanted to be close to you because i admire you and love you
i felt you did not want me near you but
allowed me to sit by you out of history or habit
i am sober now
i hope to stay sober
i hope to do all the things i dream of doing
i had dreams on drugs just like you have dreams sober
i had hopes on drugs just like you
i feel inherent shame
i have for so long
of course that is not your fault
of course that is not your fault

Welcome to the dollhouse

Eyes to the ground…
don't touch nobody…
nobody gets hurt
You're apprehensive but
Something must be alone and it's You
You salute to the sky and you backstep into hell
You fall into that category
The fire doesn't look bad but you beg to be put out
Whatever you did
To put you out
You're dead serious and
Know you're not a sociopath
When you hit something you like you
you just know it

I make a blowfish face

writing you from fox river state penitentiary
What I find troublesome
What I find hateful
I flatten into a shelf and draw the blinds
I sit in clone state
I sit forever
I sit in the reflection pool and draw a companion guide
I sit frozen and look at myself forever

I dreamed that God would be forgiving

Three charming rooms talk back and forth
enlisted for their strength and stamina
Together five sisters of addiction grow up the walls
entrusting there is no world
in which paranoia could save the two of us
Threat is infinite and jovial
Courage is a wink and a nod
Your spine is a joke
Your vertebrae are stacked snowballs
That will melt as your joints do every hour without fail
In this cruel, hot world
Where every root vegetable shrinks your dick
Where we wake up and go to work to laugh at your dick

Dewey

You marry your illness, every time
Stockholm syndrome dies harder
You pick a god figure
You work with what u have
You sink and accept the sinking
You drive a car through a fence
You mark yourself with p
Ride. You are a target and you are desired.
You liken it to drinking in the drivers seat.
The best place to have a beer.
You are clever. You are arrogant. But you are wrong.
You are a
Passenger in a drivers seat.
You undrive. You undrink.
You watch yourself die on a television
from the corner in a bar.
u smoke funny
You suck
You die

About the Author

Bunny Rogers was born in Houston, Texas, in 1990. She lives and works in New York, New York.

RUNNING

HOME

BRENDA SHAW

Matador
9 Priory Business Park,
Wistow Road, Kibworth Beauchamp,
Leicestershire. LE8 0RX
Tel: 0116 279 2299
Email: books@troubador.co.uk
Web: www.troubador.co.uk/matador
Twitter: @matadorbooks

ISBN 978 1789017 298

British Library Cataloguing in Publication Data.
A catalogue record for this book is available from the British Library.

Printed and bound in Great Britain by 4edge Limited
Typeset in 11pt Sabon by Troubador Publishing Ltd, Leicester, UK

Matador is an imprint of Troubador Publishing Ltd

To Micha'el Livni, my life partner and my best friend
without whose persistent and positive words,
nothing would have happened.

ACKNOWLEDGEMENTS

Diane Greenberg and Cassandra Melnick are irreplaceable supportive friends with well-honed professional skills as writers. They supplied endless encouragement it is thanks to their generosity that this novel was completed.

My appreciation goes to Shaul Vardi whose superb editorial skills sharpened the story.

Gary Smailes was exactly what one would want from an editor: available, wise and able to shed a fresh light on the narrative.

For I have learned to look on nature, not as in the hour of thoughtless youth, but hearing oftentimes the still, sad music of humanity.

William Wordsworth

PART ONE

LONDON
2003

ONE

Denise rushed into Graham's study, his haven where entry was by invitation only. The four-bedroom detached house, back and front garden, space for two cars in the garage, was in a North London street for the upwardly mobile middle class. His spacious study was the draw card for Graham nearly twenty years ago when he bought the house. Graham put down his pen and scowled. Bushy grey black-flecked eyebrows overhung dark eyes in their deep sockets.

"Aren't you supposed to knock? Close the door."

The door closed. Clangs from the kitchen and the faint drone of a television were silenced. A pool of light from an angled desk lamp lit papers on Graham's cherished nineteenth-century mahogany double pedestal desk.

Denise's expression made it clear she was sacrificing her valuable time. "I'm here, Dad. You said wanted to talk to me." She spoke quickly and pushed her tightly curled red hair from her face. She had not changed out of her school uniform.

Graham wanted his daughter to feel pleased that he had invited her into his retreat but the wrong words tumbled from his mouth. "Aren't you supposed to change when you get home? Your shoes are muddy. Take them off. You'll dirty the carpet."

She sniffed and moved to sit awkwardly on the edge of one of the two dark leather slingback chairs in the conversation corner. She removed her shoes and placed them precisely on the floor at her side.

Graham nodded at her and rubbed his eyes. He needed to show her that he was a busy man and that his estate agent business was thriving. With deliberate precision, he cut an advertisement from a newspaper and attached it with a paper clip to a folder.

"Dad, can we get on with it? I've got a lot of homework." Graham straightened up and rubbed the back of his neck; the top button of his white shirt was open and his striped tie was loosened.

"Denny," he scratched his nose, "I want you to buy a new outfit for Felix's bar mitzvah. You're a young lady now. I'm sure you've got your own ideas on what you like to wear." She glared at him, brown eyes glistening. "Stephanie wanted to go shopping with you but I explained to her that at sixteen you wouldn't like that."

She did not move. Graham cleared his throat.

"Don't worry about the price. Here's a bit to be getting on with and if it's not enough, let me know." He unlocked a desk drawer and pulled out a wad of notes. For a fleeting second he hoped she would spring up from the chair, put her arms round his neck and kiss his forehead.

She scratched her leg. "I'm not interested in clothes," she said, and continued to stare at him. Her pale forehead shone in the light from the standard lamp in the corner.

"Denny, I thought this would make you happy." He leant forward across the desk. *We live in the same house but in different worlds*, he thought.

"No, Dad."

"What's that supposed to mean? Tell me, Denny, is there a problem?"

She began to twist a strand of hair round her finger. She bit her lip. "I'm not coming to Felix's bar mitzvah," she whispered quickly.

"Did you say you're not coming to your brother's bar mitzvah?" He shook his head. "I can't believe what I'm hearing."

She looked at the floor. "I don't want to be there."

"You can't be serious. Felix is your brother and it's a family celebration. I've never heard of such a thing. What's got into you, Denny? You didn't used to be like this. Who's been talking to you?"

"Dad, I have a lot of homework. I don't want to discuss this. I've thought about it for a long time and I can't come."

Graham, lost for words, thumped his fist on the desk. "You owe me an explanation, Denny."

The large birthmark on the side of his neck flared when he was angry.

She stared at him and stated, "Boys have their thirteenth birthdays all the time and if they're not Jewish, no one makes a big deal about it. We're living in England in the twenty-first century. I won't say anything about the condescending attitude to Jewish girls who reach puberty."

He breathed hard. "It's our tradition. It's your tradition. Jewish boys turn thirteen and it's a big celebration. We're a Jewish family so that's what we do."

"I'm not part of this family."

He thumped the desk again. "You're my daughter, for God's sake. What's got into you, girl? This has always been your home," he shouted. The birthmark was almost purple.

"If my mother hadn't died it would have been different." She stared at him as if accusing him of murder.

He took a deep breath and walked to a cabinet on the wall behind him. He stood, back to her and breathed hard. He opened the cabinet and came back to the desk with a whisky. It was difficult for him to control his words. He spoke quietly and deliberately. "Denise, you push all the buttons, don't you? Stephanie has been a mother to you since you were two. Felix is your half-brother."

"If we were a normal family, my mother wouldn't have made a fuss like Stephanie is doing."

"We are a normal family."

"You, my stepmother and your son are the normal family. I'm the misfit."

He gulped his whisky. "Denny, that's uncalled for and not fair. It's hurtful."

"That's how you all make me feel. I don't feel like that when I'm with Oma. She hasn't been invited to the bar mitzvah. She's my mother's mother. If I'm part of the family, so is she."

"But she's not related to Felix," he blurted.

She stood up, legs astride, right hand on her hip. She announced, "If my oma is invited, I'll come." She strode out of the room.

T W O

"No, Graham, we can't change the seating plan at this stage." Stephanie sat on the stone-coloured sofa that looked as if the polythene wrap had just been removed. She sipped her late-night cup of herb tea slowly. "Graham? What's wrong? You haven't touched your digestive biscuit."

Graham, still in his shirtsleeves, was slumped in the matching armchair, his feet on a padded stone-coloured footstool with ball-in-claw wooden feet.

"If she feels like a misfit, she's only got herself to blame." Stephanie's voice grated. "Goodness only knows, I've done everything I possibly could from the day I met her."

"Everything and more, Steph. You're not to blame for this."

"You look so tired, dear. She upset you, didn't she?" She patted her short black hair. "Let me pour you a drink while I'm up."

"Not coming to her brother's bar mitzvah," he mumbled, ignoring her.

"She has to come. What will people think, Graham, if she isn't there?" Stephanie pulled her straight black skirt over her knees.

"How on earth does she get the idea that she's a misfit?" Graham mused.

"That's obvious. From that woman."

"You've said that before, Steph."

"She has been against me from the start. You remember how she was the first time you brought me to the house."

Graham was deep in his own thoughts.

"She took it for granted that she'd stay here and keep on looking after the child as if nothing had changed. You and I got married and she thought nothing would change. I had to make it very clear to her that there was no room for two women in the same house. Remember?"

"Going over the past doesn't help, Steph."

"You should phone her, Graham."

"What would I say to her?" He was alarmed.

"You could tell her we'd be delighted if she came to the synagogue service. That way she can sit with Denise, join the rest of the congregation for a glass of wine and a piece of cake afterwards, and that's the end of it. No need to mention the dinner on Sunday evening."

"It would be better if you speak to her, Steph."

"Absolutely not. She was your mother-in-law. I haven't spoken to her for fourteen years and I don't intend to change that now."

"But she'll be more likely to believe we want her to come if you phone her."

"Absolutely not."

"But—" he protested.

"Don't 'but' me, Graham. You see what's happening now, don't you?"

"What do you mean?"

"This is the way your daughter works on you. You don't see it because you always make excuses for her and we end up having an argument."

"You think she said she felt like a misfit just to get us arguing, don't you?"

"Of course she did. Whenever she can she makes trouble between you and me. It's been going on from the beginning."

"I don't agree, Steph. I think she's going through a phase. She's sixteen. It's a difficult age."

Stephanie sips her cold tea. "There you go again, making excuses for her."

"She's my daughter, Steph. I don't want her to be unhappy."

"And I'm your wife, my dear. Doesn't my happiness count?"

Graham shrugged his shoulders. "What do you want me to do?"

"I'd like you to phone the woman tomorrow and invite her to the synagogue service, like I said."

"It won't be enough for Denise. She's pushed us into a corner. She's threatened not to come if her grandmother isn't invited to the dance. Everyone will notice if she's not there."

Stephanie makes a snorting laugh. "I'll do it then. I've got an idea. I'll invite her, and at the same time, I'll make sure that she won't dare come. That way you can tell your daughter that her beloved grandmother has been invited."

THREE

"Oma, I'm here. Where are you?" Denise called.

A faint fragrance of roses filled the apartment. The hallway with its polished dark floorboards made her voice resonant. Her grandmother's keys lay on the narrow hall table, and above that hung a portrait in oils of a young woman with a serious expression. Denise threw her school bag to the floor and hung her blazer on the wooden coat rack. Vera was sitting in a rocking chair in a well-proportioned living room furnished in a mixture of styles and colours, a harmonious jumble. She had dozed off and her white curls were uncombed. Afternoon sun lit the room. She was wearing a pink hand-knitted cardigan, although the weather was warm. The newspaper had slipped to the floor.

"Oma, there you are. Let me make you a cup of tea. I woke you, didn't I? Don't get up."

Denise kissed her grandmother's forehead. "Oma, are you ill? Something's hurting. I can see it in your eyes."

"No, it's nothing, my darling. Maybe I'm getting the flu. I'm tired today, not feeling so well. How was your day?" She spoke with a faint German accent although she had lived in England for sixty-five years.

"Wait. I'll bring in the tea and then we'll talk." A clatter came from the kitchen. "Can I open the new packet of chocolate biscuits?" Denise called.

"There's some strudel in the fridge, if you want. And a carton of cream."

Denise brought in the tray and set it on the cherry-wood dining table. Vera shuffled towards the table, stopped and looked through the large window to the treetops of Highgate Wood.

"Look, Deedee. The light is so clear today."

Denise did not say anything.

"What's the matter, you look miserable. So tell me what's happening?"

"My stepmother is a witch. I want to live here with you."

Vera stirred sugar into her tea. "We've been through this before. You know all the reasons." She asked in a hushed tone. "Is this misery about the bar mitzvah?"

Denise nodded.

Vera put her hand on her granddaughter's knee. "Stephanie phoned last night to invite me. You had something to do with it? At first I didn't even recognise her voice. It's been fourteen years since we talked."

"What did she say?"

"That's between her and me."

"I told my dad I wouldn't go to the stupid dinner dance unless you were invited. And they're desperate that I go so they can show everyone how happy our family is. What did you say to her?"

"I guessed that you were behind it." Vera laughed. "You shouldn't have spoken to your father like that. There's no way I can go."

"I knew you wouldn't go. It's so ostentatious. A synagogue service is enough. Decent people would throw a small party for Felix and his friends, if he had any friends. But they spend a fortune on a splashy dinner dance just to show off. They want to show their relatives and friends that they can afford it. It makes me so angry."

"I can't be there, Deedee. I want you to go to please me, not them."

"I'm not going without you. I hate the whole idea of boys being trained like pet monkeys and then getting loads of presents just because they have their thirteenth birthday … and if you're a girl? A pat on the head and some nonsense about how it's different for girls. I'll only go if you come."

"I have to do something that I can't put off so I'm not free that weekend."

"What is it, Oma?" Denise was concerned. Vera smiled and patted her cheek. "Don't keep secrets from me."

"I have to visit someone. I'm not sure at the moment what it's all about, otherwise I would tell you. That's the only time they are free. They may have something important to tell me."

Denise began to protest.

"But you must go, Deedee. Your father will never get over it if you aren't there. There is no question of your not going. And you're to be pleasant to your father and Stephanie."

Denise pouted.

"Don't pull faces at me, you naughty girl. Do you hear what I'm telling you?"

"Do you have to be away the whole weekend, Oma?"

"Yes, darling. I won't be back and it's something I can't change."

"Who is it? You didn't say anything about them when I was here on Tuesday. Is it a relative that I haven't met?"

"I'll tell you all about it afterwards." Vera smiled, and Denise relaxed. "Now come with me. I've got something to show you."

Vera took Denise into the second bedroom. The room overlooked the next building, but a patchwork quilt with vivid patterns and bright curtains made the room inviting. Vera's canvases were stacked against the walls. There was a full-length mirror on the wardrobe door. Vera opened the wardrobe and there was a faint smell of mothballs. She took down a box from a shelf. Tissue paper rustled as she carefully drew out a sleeveless tunic. The afternoon light danced on the sheen of a deep purple silk dress.

"Try it on. I think it will fit you."

Denise looked at herself in the mirror. She gasped at her image and then held her hands to her mouth. The tunic was a classic style. She swayed slightly, watching the gentle, flowing drape of the lustrous fabric. "It's beautiful."

"It was your mother's. If you like it, it's yours. Maybe you want to wear it to the dinner dance." Vera pulled the seams. "My dressmaker can make a little alteration. The colour is as lovely on you as it was on her. She wore it to her school leaving party when she was eighteen." She sat on the narrow bed. "I have a silver chain of hers that maybe you will want to wear with it."

"It's lovely, Oma, but I'm not sure." Denise bit her lip and twisted a lock of her hair.

"Because it was your mother's?"

"It makes me feel… I mean, it's a bit creepy."

"Darling, you don't have to wear it. I just couldn't bring myself to part with it."

Denise took off the dress and laid it across her knees. She stroked the fabric and then lifted and sniffed it.

"It's been dry-cleaned, Deedee." Vera smiled.

"I felt strange when I was wearing it. I don't believe in ghosts. Do you, Oma?"

"It was nothing to do with ghosts."

"Why did I feel strange?"

"I think it's that suddenly your mother became a real person for you. A young woman who once was as alive as you are. For you, she has been no more than someone in a story, someone whose photos you have seen and you've heard about. You have no memories of her touch, her voice, her face close to yours."

Denise nodded. "I always wonder what my life would have been like if she hadn't…"

"Of course you do.'

"Especially when Stephanie shouts at me, which she does most of the time."

"And you don't make it easy for her."

"I hate her, Oma. And I hate my father for marrying her." Denise's voice was choked. "I'm so unhappy in that house."

15

She sat beside her grandmother on the spare bed, hugged her and sobbed.

"You're so cuddly."

Vera stroked her hair. "One day, you'll leave home, my pet."

"I can't wait. You should see the fuss they're making about Felix. He spends hours learning with the rabbi. Stephanie spends hours talking with the caterer and the dressmaker. If my mum had lived and I'd had a brother, she'd have made sure I was part of what was happening."

"And your mother would have insisted that you had the same celebration as the boys have when you turned thirteen."

"Would she? I didn't know that."

"She had very clear ideas about women's abilities being respected, just like men's."

"Did my father agree?"

"Sometimes they had arguments about that sort of thing. But they loved each other very much, and they adored you." Vera's pale blue eyes filled with tears. "She would have been so proud to see the young lady you've become."

Denise rubbed the dress against the skin of her face. "I love this dress." She was quiet for a moment. "I've got an idea."

"And are you going to share it with me?"

"This is what I'm thinking, Oma. All of this celebration is because Felix has turned thirteen and has come of age according to Jewish tradition. Right? As far as I'm concerned, that's complete nonsense. Don't interrupt me. I'm thinking this through as I'm telling you." She took a deep breath. "It makes sense to celebrate my coming of age, doesn't it? After all, I'm a woman. I have my periods. I could have a baby. In some countries, girls of my age are already married."

"I don't know where you're going with this, Deedee."

"It's quite simple. I will celebrate my coming of age. It will be a secret between you and me. I look amazing in this dress, don't I? I'll wear it to the dinner-dance party thing on Sunday evening. People won't recognise me at first. They'll look and they won't believe it's me. Better than that, I'll look more beautiful than Stephanie because I'm young, and even better than that… my father won't believe his eyes."

FOUR

After the service, Denise walked home from the synagogue by herself. She took a side street where there was a small children's playground. She took out her mobile and dialled her boyfriend, Kevin, who answered immediately.

"Hi," she whispered.

"Denny? Is that you? I can't hear you."

"Kev, my heart's beating fast."

"Your voice sounds weird."

"It's because my mouth is dry. I'm a bit scared."

"I am too, Denny. We don't have to do it tomorrow evening if you don't want to." He paused. "You're breathing hard."

"I could say it's because I'm excited to hear your voice, but it's really because I'm using my phone and someone who knows me might walk past."

"So what?"

"You don't understand these stupid rules because you're not Jewish. My religion forbids me to use a phone on the Sabbath."

Kevin laughed. "Does it say that in the Bible? I've noticed that there are quite a few religious rules you don't keep."

"Shut up, idiot. It's different today."

"Why? Because you went to the synagogue for once?"

"I had to, didn't I? It was my brother's big day. He's now officially a man in the eyes of the congregation. That's what the rabbi said. My skinny, spotty brother."

"And did you behave with dignity on this awesome occasion, Denny?"

She giggled. "You're making me feel better, Kev."

"I'm sorry for Felix. There he was, poor kid, with everyone watching, terrified that his voice would wobble at the crucial moment," Kevin said.

"How do you know about it?"

"I've got Jewish friends, Denny, and I went to their bar mitzvahs. Glad I didn't have to go through something like that."

"He was fine. He sang in tune. I almost felt proud of him. Hey, Kev, I didn't phone you to talk about Felix. I wanted to check that you'll be there tomorrow night."

"You're sure about this, Denny?"

"Absolutely," she whispered.

"Wow, you sound so sexy."

"See you tomorrow evening."

FIVE

Denise took her mother's dress from the row of school blouses and skirts in her wardrobe. She laid it on her bed. As she brushed her curls, she whispered to herself in the mirror, "You're looking good tonight, girl."

She grinned at her image in the full-length mirror. The coral lipstick was perfect, and she put it into the small coin-purse she would carry during the evening.

Graham shouted from downstairs. "Denise, we're leaving now. Either you come downstairs this minute or you get a taxi."

As she left her room, she pulled on a plain grey coat and threw a white cashmere stole round her neck. She ran down the stairs.

Denise left the grey coat in the cloakroom and joined the reception group, which consisted of her father, Felix and Stephanie. She stood next to her father at the entrance to the banquet hall, shaking hands and kissing cheeks. He did not look at her as she took her place.

"What kept you? Fixing your hair?" he grumbled. "You should have been here five minutes ago."

People she didn't know smiled at her and muttered congratulations. The large hall was filled with mirrors and chandeliers and a slippery parquet floor. Guests gathered around a board and easel where there was a seating plan and spoke at each other in loud voices. Tables were identically decorated with white tablecloths, gleaming silverware and floral arrangements. A band was due to begin playing when the meal was served.

"Everyone's here," Graham announced. "We can join the party." He turned towards Denise and gasped.

"Mazel tov, Dad," she said, and smiled at him.

He pulled out his handkerchief and wiped his forehead. "I'm lost for words. You look so grown up. Has Stephanie seen that dress?"

She winked at him.

"Where did my little girl go?"

She kissed his cheek and smelled his aftershave.

She joined a table with Stephanie's nieces and nephews. She went to the same school as two of them, but they were too engrossed in telling jokes to greet her. The band started playing a medley of background music. A row of waiters and waitresses emerged balancing trays of soup, and filed in choreographed rows towards their designated tables. Denise waited a few minutes until soupspoons reached mouths. No one noticed her creep away.

Kevin was waiting for her in the car park. He was a sixth-form student at the local grammar school who had just got his driver's licence and now earned pocket money by delivering groceries for his father's gourmet food shop. He was a gentle and funny youth, tall and thin, with hands a size too large. Three months ago when they started walking home together through the park, he had been shy and tentative, but that had changed.

She climbed into the grocery van.

"Where to, Denny?" he joked.

"My place, of course. Up the stairs and second door on the left." She could not stop laughing. "Drive fast and don't argue. They won't be back for at least two hours. They're drinking soup. There are four courses and the speeches to get through."

"Did anyone see you leave?"

"I don't think so, and if they saw me leave the hall, they'd just think I was going to the toilet. Don't be nervous."

Kevin parked the van ten doors away from the house. "Are you sure this is all right, Denny?"

They ran upstairs, silent on the carpeted stairs.

"This house is so big, Denny."

She took his hand. "Close your eyes, Kev. I'm taking you into my room. Sit down there and keep your eyes closed."

A few seconds passed.

"Now open them."

Her room at the back of the house was lined with posters of Venus and Serena Williams. A bookcase above her desk held schoolbooks and novels. On the top shelf stood the shields and cups that proclaimed Denise's athletic talent.

The room was lit by candles, and on the desk was a tray with a single rose, a bottle of cava, two wine glasses and a condom. She took off the grey overcoat. Kevin gasped and sat on the double bed that Denise had covered with a bath sheet.

"Wow, Den."

They kissed, and he unzipped her dress.

Afterwards they stood in the kitchen, drinking water and kissing.

"We'd better leave. They might come back any minute."

"We're safe for at least another hour."

"I jump every time I hear a car in the street."

"Relax, Kev. There's one more thing I want to do while we've got the house to ourselves."

She took a key from a hook in the kitchen.

"Come with me. I want to see what my father's got in his secret hideaway."

She unlocked the door of Graham's study. "I'm only allowed in here by invitation. He keeps it locked all the time and he spends hours in here in the evenings."

She switched on the desk light.

"Looks like an estate agent's office to me," said Kevin. "All those books about property law and all those files."

"This is the drinks cabinet," she said. "Fancy a whisky?"

"Denny, this is crazy. Let's go."

"In a minute, Kev. I want to see what he keeps in the drawers of his desk."

"You shouldn't do that."

She sprang the lock on the middle drawer with a paper knife. "Certificates. Births, deaths, marriages." She began piling the papers in their folders on the desktop. "Hey, Kevin, this folder's got my mum's name on it."

Inside the folder there was a newspaper cutting: *The Jewish Chronicle*, October 1987. The two of them, heads touching, read:

A British tourist, killed in the bomb attack at the Jerusalem Café two days ago, has been named as Gabriella Levisohn. She was due to fly back to England only four hours after the attack...

They sat in Kevin's father's van in the car park near the school. Denise's face was white under the street lamp.

"Lies. Why did they tell me lies?"

"You said she was killed in a traffic accident on the M1."

"That's what they've always told me. My dad. My grandmother. They lied to me. She was my mother. Aren't I entitled to know what happened to her?" she shouted.

"Calm down, Denny. You won't find out anything by yelling."

"Don't you understand a thing, Kev? It's bad enough they lied to me. What's worse is that no one ever told me that my mother went to Israel. I was seven months old. Who'd leave a seven-month-old baby and go off to a war zone, a crazy country where terrorists throw bombs into cafés? She didn't care about me. It's like she wanted to get herself killed."

"Denny, you're hysterical. You're off the wall."

S I X

Two weeks previously, Vera had had a sleepless night. She gazed into the shades of darkness through the large window of her flat in the converted Victorian house. The outline of the trees of Highgate Wood formed a horizon as precise as a paper cut. The moon was full and the night sky had a faint pearly shade. The silhouette of an owl flew across with its soft, slow wing beats. She felt a pang of fear, and then suddenly she was dizzy. She staggered to the sofa.

When she opened her eyes, it was daylight and she was still lying on the sofa. There was a metallic taste in her mouth and a large patch of dried blood on one of the cushions. She phoned her lifelong friend Elizabeth, who was a retired family doctor.

"I'm frightened, Elizabeth."

"Of course you are," Elizabeth said. "First we have to find out what is wrong, and then we will find out what can be done. I need to make a few phone calls."

Now Vera was by herself in the spotless hospital room. A blackbird sang outside and the wind blew leaves against the paned window. Her throat was sore and she wanted to fall asleep, but the nurse had told her that the surgeon was on his way. Elizabeth had arranged her admission to a private hospital, saying, "The National Health Service is falling to pieces and this is urgent."

The surgeon, wearing his scrubs, looked as if he had not left school. "We removed some tissue that was causing a small blockage. It's been sent to the laboratory as a routine measure."

His avoidance of eye contact was more convincing than his words. She asked him, "Is it cancer?"

"At this stage," he answered in a gentle tone, "it's impossible to be certain."

Vera's son, Peter, a pathologist at the Manchester Royal Infirmary, arrived that afternoon. He was a tall man with an unsmiling, bony face, deep-set eyes and a receding hairline. He leaned over to kiss her forehead.

"You seemed fine when you were with us a month ago, Mum. When did you notice that you had a problem?"

"I've had indigestion for years, so I didn't notice anything until a few weeks ago when it got difficult to swallow."

He nodded.

"I should have told you about it."

"You called Elizabeth. She's got more local connections than I have. You did the right thing."

She stroked his hand. "Thank you for coming, Peter."

They sat in silence for a few minutes.

"Help me sip a little water," she said. "Be honest with me, Peter. What's going on?"

Peter sat on the bed. He was wearing jeans and a thick, navy blue turtleneck sweater. He spoke as if considering each word.

"First of all," he said, "the diagnosis has probably been made. The doctors will tell you about the treatment options when they think you are ready." He continued after another long pause. "I'll be with you when they visit. Whatever they find, I will be here for you and do everything I can to make sure you have the best treatment."

"I've had a full life, Peter, and I want to go peacefully. Will you explain to the surgeons that I just want to be kept as comfortable as possible and let nature take its course?"

"I hear you, Mum."

"But there is one thing." She found it hard to talk for long. "Will you promise me to do what is best for Deedee? It's going to be awful for her at that house. They'll try to stifle her. She's got to get away. It's not going to be easy for her. I've organised a place for her at a sixth-form college in the Lake District. I'm sure that it will be the right environment for her. But her father and that wife of his won't want her to leave London."

"She's sixteen and they'll have the law on their side."

"But surely with teenagers of sixteen, wouldn't her wishes be considered?"

"That's a question for a lawyer."

"Peter," it was more comfortable for her to whisper, "at least do what you can to get her to stay with you and your family during the summer holidays."

"Of course I will. She'll get on with our kids and

she'll love where we live. We've invited her so many times over the years."

"I know. I think they're worried that you and Margot will contaminate her."

"They're right, aren't they, Mum? She'll come to us and eat non-kosher food. She'll discover that Margot is good fun to be with even if she isn't Jewish, and that's it. She'll slide down the slippery slope and out of the tribe."

"Peter, don't make me laugh. It hurts."

"I like to see that twinkle in your eyes, Mum. I want to check with my colleagues at the infirmary to see if you would get better treatment up north. And it goes without saying that if you want, you can move into the house with Margot, me and the kids."

"Peter, I'm not planning to end my days in Greater Manchester."

SEVEN

Denise arrived after school on the day of her grandmother's discharge from hospital. Vera was sitting in her rocking chair in the living room, wearing the baggy pink cardigan. A faded pink blanket was thrown over her lap. Denise kissed her forehead and then sat on the floor, hugging her knees.

"Oma, I'll make tea in a minute. You should have seen my dad's face when he saw me in the dress. He couldn't believe his eyes. The bar mitzvah was completely and utterly boring. I knew about ten people and I wouldn't want to spend more than ten seconds with any of them."

Actually, I didn't spend more than ten seconds with them, but there are some things I'm not telling you about, Oma, she thought.

"And what a waste of food. Honestly, who could eat a meal like that, starting at eight o'clock in the evening? And you should have seen what some of the women were wearing: short skirts stretched over their big bottoms. Are you all right, Oma? You're so pale. What is it?"

"I haven't got over the flu. I'll be fine in a few days."
She added, "To see you like this makes me feel better."

"Who's the man talking on the phone in the kitchen?"

Peter strode into the room. "Hello, Denise. I'm your Uncle Peter."

They stared at each other, and then they both began to laugh.

"Ridiculous, isn't it?" he said. "Your oma's very tired and I've told her to go and rest, but she wanted to see you first."

When Vera was in bed sleeping, Peter and Denise talked in the living room.

"She's very ill, Denise." His voice was deep.

"Can't she have treatment?" she asked.

"She could have an operation but there's no guarantee it would make her better. She doesn't want it."

"How bad – I mean, what's going to happen?"

"She may only be with us for a few months at most. She wants to stay at home as long as she can."

"What can I do?" She struggled to hold back her tears.

"Be with her whenever you can."

"You're my Uncle Peter? I've always wanted to meet you."

"You're welcome any time you want to stay with us in our big, untidy house outside Manchester."

"My dad and my stepmother won't let me come."

"That's a shame because you've got a pair of cousins who want to meet you. You'd have a great time together."

As Graham drove Denise home from her grandmother's, she asked him to pull over because she wanted to talk to him before they got to the house.

"I know you won't like this, Dad, but I have to talk to you about Oma."

Graham ran his finger between his collar and his neck.

"Just listen to me, Dad. She's very ill. I think she's going to die."

"Don't be melodramatic."

"I'm not making this up, Dad."

"Who's taking care of her?"

"My Uncle Peter. From Manchester."

"Is he there at the house? Did you meet him?" Graham pursed his lips and snorted.

"He's nice. I like him. Why didn't you and Stephanie let me stay with him and his family in the school holidays? I kept asking."

"We thought you wouldn't get on. You kept asking because your grandmother told you to."

"That's not true. They're my cousins and I've always wanted to meet them."

"We talked about it and decided they wouldn't be a good influence."

"You and Stephanie talked about it? What do you mean, 'wouldn't be a good influence'? He's a doctor. She's a social worker. They've got kids around my age."

"You've got other cousins around your age."

"Stephanie's sister's kids. I don't like them and they don't like me."

"If you must know, Denny, we had a big argument years ago."

"You and Uncle Peter? What was it about?"

"It's none of your business, Denny. Why do you keep pushing?"

"It was about my mother, wasn't it?" she said loudly. Her eyes were blazing.

"Is that what your uncle told you just now?"

"No. I'm guessing. He was her brother. There's something you're not telling me, and you're scared I'll find out if I get to know him better."

"Don't be so ridiculous, Denny. You know what happened to your mother. No one has ever hidden that from you."

"I know what you told me. But how do I know if that's the truth?"

"Why would I lie to you, Denny?" The birthmark on his neck was flaring, and he stared straight ahead.

"People lie to their kids. I know kids who only found out they were adopted by accident. Their adoptive parents never told them."

"I've had just about enough of this, Denny. We're going home." He started the car.

"You bury your head in the sand, Graham Levisohn. Do you think that if you don't talk about these things, you'll suddenly have the most perfect family in North London? You're being horrible to me, Dad, and you tell me that you love me. If you loved me, you'd try to understand what I'm going through. Go home on your own. I'm taking the bus."

He put his hand on her wrist. "There's something I should tell you. It's about Stephanie and your grandmother."

"I want to know, Dad."

He switched off the car engine again.

"Stephanie thought it best that…" He stopped talking and ran his tongue over his lips.

"Go on, Dad."

"She wanted you to think of her as your mother. She thought it would be best for you and for me. And then, if we were to have a child together, we'd bring you both up as a normal family."

"Oma looked after me until you married Stephanie, didn't she?"

"Yes."

"Why didn't you let me see her for years?"

"I've told you. We thought it would be complicated if there were two children in the family and they had different grandmothers. We did it for good reasons, Denny."

"It was a lie. You brought me up to believe a lie." She almost spat.

"I'm sorry you see it like that. I'm very sorry."

"Being sorry doesn't make up for telling me lies, or for the miserable years my oma had because you wouldn't let me see her."

They stopped talking. It was raining lightly and beginning to get dark.

"What other lies have you told me, Dad? That's what I ask myself."

"Denny, I've said I'm sorry. Maybe we made a mistake. But you spend time with your grandmother now."

"While she's still with us." Denise opened her mouth as if to speak again, but then was quiet.

"Can we go home now, Denise?"

"I have one more question." The words tumbled out.

"Go ahead."

"Where was my mother going when she died, Dad?"

He took a deep breath. "What difference does it make, Denny?"

"I just want to know."

"She was on the way home from Manchester. It was terrible. I can't bear to talk about it any more."

That's absolutely not true, Dad, she thought. *What are you covering up?*

"Let's go home," she said.

EIGHT

Vera lay on the sofa in the living room. Denise put her grandmother's hand to her cheek.

"Oma, your hand is cold and your rings are loose. I remember your hands from when I was eight and I started coming to visit you. They were warm and soft. And you always had paint under some of your nails. And you were warm and lovely to hug, but now you're getting too thin. Your wedding ring was never loose like this. I've never asked you about my grandfather."

Vera became tired quickly, but she had much to tell.

"Erich was much older than me and he had been married before. Such terrible things happened in Europe in those years, Deedee. His first wife and his two children were taken and he never knew what happened to them. He managed to get to England and he tried to get them out of Austria…" She paused. "He was kind to me, but he pined for them until the day he died."

Vera rested against the cushions. "I suppose that for him, I was more a daughter than a wife. He had been a violinist, but he never played again once he left Vienna.

He came to London where he thought he had no one, but a distant cousin found him and gave him work in his pharmacy.

"The children, your mother and your Uncle Peter, upset him and he would shout at them. They were good children, so sweet when they were small. I thought they would console him. I didn't understand why he shouted at them. Now I think they must have reminded him of the children he lost."

She stopped and sipped some hot water. "We couldn't talk about things, and he went more and more into himself. I became miserable and angry. So you see, my darling, we were two good people who were making each other's lives unhappy. Erich suggested that we divorce while I was still a young woman. He said he was finished and he wanted me to find someone who could make me happy."

She paused again and twisted her wedding ring. "He and his cousin bought this house and had it converted into flats. He always made sure I wouldn't have to worry about money. Once we were divorced, it was easier for us to talk and, though it may sound strange, we became good friends. He was like an uncle with the children. He would buy them presents and take them out somewhere for a treat, but he couldn't bear to be with them for very long. It took me time to begin to understand that his wounds could never heal. He did what he could by becoming a father and providing for his family. Erich died about five years after the divorce."

"What did he look like?"

"He was tall, and your uncle looks like him. He waved his arms a lot when he talked. I told him once that he should have been a conductor rather than a violinist, which made him smile. Not many things did."

They were watching a soap opera on TV. Denise asked, "Is it a good time now to tell me how my parents met?"

"I was waiting for you to ask me." Vera smiled and spoke slowly. "Gabriella went to Spain on an archaeological dig when she was a student. She told me that she was in a bar in Barcelona the evening before she was due to come home. There was a small group of English tourists, drinking and talking about their wonderful cheap holiday on the Costa Brava. She went up to them and asked whether they thought it was a good idea to support Spanish tourism. She was never shy. It was still Franco's Spain. You know what I'm talking about?"

Denise nodded.

"Apparently they just shrugged their shoulders and said, 'So what? It's cheap and there's plenty of booze.' I think your father fell in love at first sight. Maybe he realised that she was Jewish. He asked her where she was from. He invited her to meet up with him when they were back in London so that they could have a proper discussion about Franco. It was just an excuse, of course. She told me about him. She said he was kind, that he was very bright and interested in a lot of things, but hadn't managed to finish university because of some family problems."

"Did you like him when you met him?"

"I thought he was either shy or he was trying to hide something about himself. He loved Gabriella very much, you know. I think his parents didn't like her. They were peculiar people."

"Were you happy when they married?" She fidgeted.

"If my daughter was happy, then I was happy too. What's this about, Deedee?"

"I found out something. I can't tell you how I found out."

Vera pulled herself up so she was sitting. "You and I are never to have secrets. You agree?"

Denise stroked her grandmother's cold hand. "I found out that my mother was killed by a terrorist bomb in Jerusalem."

Vera pulled her hand away. "Your mother and your uncle were brainwashed. They wasted hours with that Zionist youth group. That's all they ever talked about."

"Didn't you ever want to live in Israel, Oma?"

Vera looked annoyed. "Me? Why on earth should I want to live there? This country took me in and gave me a life. Never forget that, Denny. This is a safe and stable place to live."

"But, Oma,…" Denise began.

"Bring me some warm water, my pet."

When Denise came back with the water, Vera said, "Deedee, I don't want to know what you found out about your poor mother's death – what is past is over. Her life finished and you are only just beginning yours. That's all that matters. You're a talented young woman; intelligent and athletic. You'll succeed in whatever you choose to do with your life. I'm doing everything I can to give you a chance you wouldn't otherwise have. I'm telling you to get on with your life. Do your best, always. It's what your mother did, and it's what she would want for you."

"But, Oma, I only want—"

"I know what you want to know, and I'm telling you that worrying about the past is a waste of time and energy."

Denise shrugged. "That's what you say, but I'm angry. Can't you understand that? Why did she deliberately go to a dangerous place when she had a young baby? I keep thinking about it. I feel like she abandoned me."

"What nonsense you talk, Deedee."

"She chose a dangerous country over her own baby daughter."

"Of course you're angry that your mother passed away. You have every right to be. It's painful to talk about. Being angry is natural when someone dies. You know logically that she would never have willingly abandoned you. But in your heart, you are still the poor baby that you were, crying for your mother."

"You aren't going to tell me why she was in Jerusalem, are you, Oma?"

"I'm tired, my pet. I need to sleep for a while."

NINE

"The letter is from a lawyer who says that Vera Baumgarten wants to meet with us," Graham said to Stephanie as they finished breakfast.

"I know what it's about and I have no intention of going," Stephanie replied.

As usual, Graham swallowed a flash of annoyance. "How can you know, Stephanie?"

"You are so naive when it comes to your daughter," Stephanie retorted. "That woman has been planning this for years. She worked on Denise while we were away. All this stuff about being ill is a way of convincing Denise that she has to stay with her because she's helping a poor old, sick woman. If you had listened to me, you would have insisted on her coming with us. Look what happened when we got back from Italy. You went round to collect her, and what did she say to you?"

"She said she didn't want to come back immediately because her grandmother had a doctor's appointment the next day."

"Do you know if it's true? Can you ever find out if it's true? I don't believe she's any sicker than I am."

"You don't know and neither do I. You're getting yourself all worked up. The lawyer says he's known Vera all his life and that it was in Denise's best interests that we meet." Graham spoke slowly.

"He's just threatening us. We've got our own lawyer."

"I've already asked him to come to the meeting."

"In that case," Stephanie insisted, "I'll come if the meeting is held in his office, not theirs."

Small victory, thought Graham. *Worth the fight.*

Martin had an office in the suite of a large law firm in West London. The room was wood panelled, and lithographs of pastoral scenes from the eighteenth century were an apology for decoration. There were stacks of files with papers spilling out over his huge desk.

Martin was a short man with a shiny dome, across which straddled lonely strands of black hair. Vera was there in a wheelchair, looking frail. Her friend Elizabeth and a youngish man Stephanie thought she recognised sat on one of the two matching rich chestnut-coloured Chesterfield sofas, with Graham and Stephanie opposite.

The young man stood up and moved to stand next to Vera. There was something of the athlete about him. He leaned forward slightly as he spoke, as if he was clutching a tennis racket and waiting for the opponent's serve.

"You already know Vera. This is my mother, Dr Elizabeth Klein. She and Vera have been close friends since they came to England as child refugees with the *Kindertransport* over sixty years ago. My name is

41

Terence, and I'm a family lawyer. I will speak for Vera, who as you know is very ill."

Stephanie suddenly remembered where she had seen Terence before. It was years ago in the family court, soon after she and Graham had married. He had been Vera's lawyer. Vera had been impossible, Stephanie recalled. The woman couldn't see how confused little Denise would be if she kept seeing her grandmother. It was so obvious that any child needs a mother more than a grandmother. *In the end, our lawyer had to spell out clearly that she could only see the child if we agreed. Of course we didn't.* The memory was still vivid.

Stephanie whispered to Graham, "You remember who that man, Terence, is, don't you?"

Graham told her to keep quiet. She was annoyed.

Terence paused and cleared his throat. "I'll quickly give the background. Vera took care of Denise when she was a baby following her mother's untimely death. She moved into Graham's home and stayed there until Stephanie arrived. Graham and Stephanie decided that it would be best for Denise if they were to forbid Vera to have access to her grandchild. Eight years ago, however, contact between grandmother and granddaughter was renewed and there has been a strong bond between them ever since."

Stephanie sighed, and Graham squeezed her hand. Vera waved her hand at Terence. He bent over so she could whisper into his ear.

Terence explained, "Vera has written what she wants to say in a letter to Graham. The subject of the letter is Denise's future. While she still has a little strength, Vera wants to be part of a discussion about the girl's best interests. She dictated this to me over a number of hours. So, with everyone's permission, I'll go ahead and read it."

Martin addressed Graham. "I've read it and I think you'll agree that a meeting at this time was good idea."

"We are Denise's parents and it is for us to decide what is in her best interests, as we have done up till now," Stephanie blurted out.

Terence ignored her interruption. "The letter is addressed to Graham, and is as follows."

Dear Graham,

You were my son-in-law and you are my granddaughter's father. As you can see, I am ill, and I know that I do not have long to live. I have given myself the privilege of saying in front of witnesses what I need to say to you at this time. My dearest wish is that this will be the day that we will all be able to let go of past differences and talk about how to help Denise through the next phase of her life.

I did not wish to be separated from Denise when she was a small child, but as you know, that is what happened. The relationships between us could have been different. I tried to reach out to Stephanie, and maybe I did this in the wrong way. I take some of the responsibility for the estrangement between us. I was hurt by the decision you both made all those years ago to forbid me to see my granddaughter. The only consolation I had then was the assumption that both of you loved Denise and did what you thought was best for her. She found her own way back to me when she was still a young child. This is not the place to describe the pleasure of being part of her life over the last eight years. The fact that she is developing into such a fine young woman indicates that you have given her a good home in which to grow up. I forgive you for what you did. I have done all I can to show her that your home is also her home.

She is now sixteen biologically mature but not legally permitted to make her own decisions. You and I know that she has been making her own decisions since she was very young. The two of us share a privileged knowledge of who she is and where she came from. Her sharp intelligence is similar to her mother's. She is talented in many areas, but naturally at her age she is not fully aware of what she might achieve. We know something about her prickly personality and her obstinacy.

She and I have grown very close and soon she will have to cope with another loss. My intention when I invited both of you here today was that we would be able at last to bridge our differences and have a discussion about Denise's future.

I have made a clause in my will regarding a sixth-form boarding college for her further education. I believe this is what she wants, and I also believe she will benefit greatly from a boarding environment.

Thank you for listening to me.

Vera.

Elizabeth opened her handbag and took out a neatly folded handkerchief.

Graham cringed. It should not have come to this. He should never have listened to Stephanie. It was a long time ago but the guilt was a perpetual ache in his chest.

Stephanie broke the silence. "What I would like to know is what my daughter has been doing at Vera's home for the last month? Has she been taking care of her? If Vera's condition is as serious as she says, she should be in hospital. It is totally unsuitable for a girl of sixteen to be exposed to a dying woman. Has my daughter had the responsibility for her nursing care? There is no way we, her parents, would have given her permission to stay there if we had been correctly informed." She paused and looked at Martin.

"Let me handle this," Graham whispered to Stephanie.

Terence intervened. "Denise has not been involved in any of Vera's nursing care. Vera asked for my help. As she says in her letter, she wanted to be able to sit with you and talk through the problems you will soon be facing."

Stephanie stood up and straightened her skirt. "The letter is addressed to my husband. The possibility that I, as the girl's mother, might be able to comfort and advise her is completely ignored. I see no point in staying here." She swept out of the room, while Graham looked to Martin, who shrugged.

"Excuse me for a moment," Graham said as he left the room.

Stephanie was sitting on an overlarge leather armchair in the foyer. Her eyes were red.

"It's intolerable, Graham. What did she say about forgiving us? How dare she? It was she who always wanted to interfere in the way I was bringing up our daughter."

Graham stroked her hand. "It's best that you come back into the room, Steph. It won't look good if you don't. We're here to discuss Denise, and you're here because you're her mother. I'll explain that you hadn't realised how ill Vera was and it shocked you. Come on, Steph. Fix your face and let's go back together."

Arm in arm, they returned to Martin's office and Stephanie nodded graciously towards Terence, who said, "Vera wants Denise to be given the chance to decide for herself whether she continues at her present school or transfers to a sixth-form boarding college."

Stephanie gasped. "She's a child. How on earth can she decide for herself?"

"She's sixteen, and any judge will listen carefully to what she has to say," Martin said.

"I thought the legal age for adult decisions was eighteen," Stephanie retorted.

"I think that is why Vera wanted us to meet. It will be much easier for Denise if all the adults that are close to her agree," Martin explained.

Vera waved again at Terence, who bent down to listen to her whisper.

"Vera would like to hear what you have to say, Stephanie."

Stephanie stood up. "I've been a mother to Denise for the last fourteen years. Graham and I are rightly proud of all that she has achieved. We've made sure that she feels loved at home and secure at school. The proof that we have been good parents is obvious. She's a top student and a prizewinning athlete. It would obviously be stressful for her to change schools. She would have to make new friends and adjust to new teachers. As for moving away from home to a boarding school… well, that speaks for itself, doesn't it? Vera is a sick woman, and it is sad that she thinks she may not live much longer. But these things happen all the time. Denise is fortunate that she still has two parents who love her. We won't agree to this. Why should we even consider a boarding school?"

As she sat down, Graham asked, "If we have to let Denise decide, how will this be organised? Who will give her the choices?"

"Terence and I will explain it to her," Martin said.

Stephanie was furious. Red spots blazed on her cheeks. "You've set this up, all of you. You've made Graham and me look like fools. I know whose work this is." She turned to face Vera and waved her index finger. "It's yours, Vera. For years you have been doing everything you can to win Denise's affection and make her despise her parents."

Terence shifted in his chair. "Graham, I realise now that Martin and I should have prepared you for this meeting, and I apologise."

When they arrived home, Graham marched into his study and Stephanie joined him before he could close the door. She said angrily, "Your problem, Graham, is that you don't face up to what's going on under your nose."

He turned his back to her as he poured himself a whisky. "You shouldn't have left the room like that. It looked very bad." *She's going to tell me that she and her mother saw that this was going to happen*, he thought to himself.

"You don't get it, do you?" she continued. "That woman will leave a will. There will be an executor. What she did today was to tell us that she'll have the last word. It will be her way, either amicably, which is what she tried today, or through the lawyers. She's won, don't you see? She always wanted to get Denise away from me. It's just like my mother said."

"You're being ridiculous. Denise is only sixteen. We're her parents."

"If Denise decides she wants to leave us, there's nothing we'll be able to do about it. The law will be on her side. That's the way it is with teenagers these days."

Graham breathed heavily and gritted his teeth. "What do you want me to do, Steph?"

"I want you to tell her where she'll live and where she'll go to school. It's not for her to decide these things, and you have to make that clear to her."

"Steph, she's a young woman, not a child. Look at her."

"And you're her father. You make the decision and then you tell her. You don't have a discussion about things like this with children."

Graham stared at her as if she was a stranger. "Haven't you noticed that she lives her own life here?" he shouted. "She may be living under our roof, but she comes and goes as she pleases. Do you know where she

48

goes all the time? Do you know any of her friends? Does she have a boyfriend? When was the last time she talked to you about anything?"

"And you, Graham?" Stephanie responded with a chill in her voice. "You've spent half your life as her chauffeur. Does she talk to you in the car? You always take her side against me."

"That's not fair." Graham slammed his fist on the desk.

"She plays with you, Graham. She can get whatever she wants out of you."

"It's not a game, Steph. It's our family."

"Our family?" she mocked. "It's never been *our* family. It's always been you and your beloved daughter against Felix and me. I'm going round to my mother's."

TEN

Graham must have dozed off. The telephone on his desk woke him. It was nine o'clock at night. He didn't recognise the voice. His left arm was numb because he had been lying on it.

"It's Rabbi Mannheim speaking, Graham. This is a delicate matter and I'd prefer to discuss it with you personally. Could I come to your house now?"

"Rabbi, what is it about? I'm not feeling well at the moment."

"I would like a few minutes of your time to talk with you about your daughter."

Graham, only half awake, agreed. Fifteen minutes later, the front doorbell chimed and the portly rabbi in his homburg hat asked if he could come in.

"I'll get straight to the point," he said in faintly accented English, his head slightly tilted to indicate sympathy. "This is a sad, not to say tragic, loss for all of you, but especially for your daughter."

Graham still felt groggy. The house was quiet. Where was everybody?

"Wait, Rabbi. I'm not sure I understand."

"Your mother-in-law passed away around four this afternoon."

"But we were with her this morning," Graham said.

The rabbi shook his hand and touched his shoulder. "Apparently she had been taken to a meeting. When she got back home she suddenly collapsed. Her passing was swift and peaceful." He stopped talking. Sweat broke out on Graham's forehead. "Please accept my condolences. I apologise for bringing sad news, but I was sure someone would have told you."

"Rabbi, my wife must be upstairs. I think she should join us."

Graham ran upstairs to find Stephanie before he remembered that she had gone with Felix to her mother's. He did not know where Denise was.

"My wife had to visit her mother," he explained.

Rabbi Mannheim cleared his throat. "Vera Baumgarten was not a member of our congregation, but her daughter, your late wife Gabriella, was. I officiated at your wedding, as you will remember. Such a terrible tragedy that only two years later she was taken from you."

Graham cleared his throat.

"Thank God you have the consolation of your daughter. This is what I wanted to talk about with you, Mr Levisohn."

"Thank you for your concern, Rabbi. Denise is not home at the moment." *And I have no idea where she is*, he thought. *What kind of father am I?* He rubbed the back of his neck. "My wife and I will do everything we can to comfort her."

"Of course. But I have a question to ask you." The rabbi nodded before he continued, "I have been told that Vera wished to be cremated. As you know, cremation of the body is against Orthodox Jewish practice. However, comforting the bereaved is a central commandment. If you agree, I will attend the cremation and speak to Denise."

"Yes, Rabbi. It's very kind of you. Certainly my wife and I have no objection."

"And now, I won't waste any more of your time. Goodnight, Mr Levisohn."

As he closed the door on the rabbi, Graham's stomach churned. Stephanie would be furious if he went to the crematorium. But who was she to keep dictating how he related to his daughter? *My poor daughter*, he thought, *she'll have to go through the ordeal of the funeral on her own.* He would be there for her, he decided.

There were more people than he expected at Golders Green Crematorium. Vera's former colleagues and students from the school where she had taught art history for years came to pay their respects. Graham stood near the back, wearing sunglasses although it was a cloudy day. Denise looked fragile, her white face contrasting with her dark dress, her red hair covered with a black scarf. The tall man next to her would be Peter, Gabriella's brother, the doctor from Manchester. Elizabeth and Terence stood on her other side. There was organ music, and some brief eulogies. Graham saw Denise flinch as the coffin slipped behind the heavy curtain. People approached the mourners and he saw the rabbi talking to Denise. The crowd was beginning to move towards the car park, but he stood rooted to the spot. Denise walked towards him and stood in front of him.

"It means a lot to me that you came," she said. He reached out to hold her, but she had already turned away from him.

Out in the car park, Peter strode purposefully towards him.

"Sorry about your mother. I wish you long life," Graham said as he shook Peter's hand.

Peter broke the silence. "Where's Denise going to go?" he said in that deep voice that Graham remembered.

"What kind of a question is that? She'll come home, of course."

"Graham, this is awful for her. She won't make it easy for you and Stephanie."

"What's that got to do with you?"

"She's my niece, Graham. She's got cousins, my kids, who are about her age and they're Vera's grandchildren, too. Why don't you let her stay with us for the rest of the summer holidays?"

"I'm her father," Graham snapped. "It's up to me to decide."

"This is a tough time for her, Graham."

"What's that got to do with you? She has a home. She has parents. So keep out of it."

Peter spoke in that measured voice of his. "She's staying with my mother's friend Elizabeth. She refuses to go home. She thought you wouldn't come to the cremation, Graham. It means everything to her that you're here. She's not running away from you."

"Since you know where she is, tell her to come home."

"She wants to come back to Manchester with me."

Graham raised his voice. A couple passing by stopped for a moment and listened.

"It's not up to her or to you to decide. I'm her father and I make the decisions for her. Haven't I made that clear enough?"

"Graham, think about it from her point of view. She's sixteen. She's heartbroken, and at that age she needs to be with others of her own age. Let her be with her cousins. They loved their grandmother too."

"Not unless Stephanie agrees. We're her parents," he growled.

"You're her father and my sister was her mother, to be accurate."

"It's none of your damned business." He began to stride towards his car.

Peter caught up with him. "I don't agree. She's my niece and she's had more than her fair share of bereavements. Let her have a change of scenery. She'll come with me anyway, whatever you and Stephanie say. We both know that. Let her come with your agreement."

"She's my daughter and I'll make the decisions," Graham repeated.

"I doubt that."

PART TWO

ANOTHER
ENGLAND
2003 TO 2008

ELEVEN

Peter took a medical journal from his briefcase as soon as the train left Euston. He scanned the contents and smoothed the page several times, but did not read.

Denise wanted him to talk to her, to ask her questions, to notice that she was there. She kept shivering although she was not cold. She wanted to cry but tears would not come. It was difficult to breathe easily. She stared out of the window at the outlines of houses and the dark, steely sky. From the train, she could glimpse other people's lives. Television screens flickered. A boy was hunched over his computer. A woman was angry with a child. *Everyone else has a family and a home*, she thought. *I'm just a piece of torn wrapping paper that's been thrown to the wind.*

Peter suddenly blew his nose loudly and wiped his eyes with a large handkerchief. He cleared his throat. "We're not a very conventional lot and the house is often a bit of a mess. You won't mind that, will you?"

She shrugged. "You never saw my room, did you? Must run in the family."

There was another long silence, apart from the regular clatter of the train on the tracks.

Margot met them at Piccadilly Station. She was slightly built and about the same height as Denise. Her eyes were like blackcurrants. Her grey hair was pulled back into a ponytail and she was wearing a plum-coloured tracksuit. "What a terrible day you've had, Denise. I've thought of you for years as Deedee because that's what Vera always called you. She talked about you all the time when she stayed with us. How was the journey?"

She took Denise's arm and led her through the station.

"Welcome to Manchester. Kingdom of the raincoat," she announced. "Rob and Nic are at the house. They're very excited about you coming. You haven't ever met them, have you. They wanted to come to meet you, but I thought it might be too much and you'd most likely be tired. I hope you don't mind. It's about a half-hour drive at this time of day. We're outside the city in a village called Littleborough. What did you bring with you? We've put out things for you in case you forgot something. Here's the car."

She paused for breath. Denise could not place her accent. Sometimes she sounded French and at other times she sounded Mancunian. Margot continued with her questions. Was Denise hungry? Had she ever been to Manchester before? *She's the talker and Peter's the silent one*, Denise thought. She liked the hug they had given each other at the station.

The doors of the double garage were open and Margot drove in. Bikes leaned against each other and there were canvas bags, ropes and boots on wide shelves. A canoe was suspended from the ceiling. The car was a Land Cruiser and it was streaked with mud.

"I'll show you round tomorrow," Margot said, as they went into the house. "Peter and I wanted a large, old house not too far from the city. We didn't manage to produce enough children to fill it, so you've got a choice of rooms if you don't like the one we've fixed up for you."

They went up the wooden staircase. "The kids thought you'd like this room. The house is Victorian and this could have been an extra sitting room. If it's not raining in the morning, you can look past our neglected garden and convince yourself that you're seeing the Dales."

The words *Welcome Denby* were scattered in different colours and styles over a piece of poster board pinned to the door. Coloured balloons and streamers bobbed from the ceiling. The double bed had a patchwork quilt, and a reading lamp stood on the bedside table next to a small pile of paperbacks. There was a tiled fireplace, brass fire irons and a mantelpiece with framed photos of Oma as a young woman; her husband, Erich; and Peter and Gabriella as children. An old wooden rocking chair stood near the fireplace.

"We'll be downstairs in the kitchen. Follow the smells and join us if you want to, but if you don't feel like it tonight, we'll understand."

Denise wanted to meet her cousins but she felt drained. *I've had enough for one day, she thought.* She undressed slowly and lay on the bed, listening to the rain pattering on the window and the faint sound of someone practising the flute.

She fell asleep and woke startled, with a sense that someone was in the room. "Who's there?" she called out. No one answered, and she turned on the bedside lamp. She felt afraid. The house was quiet and she did not know what time it was. As she got out of bed, a silky black cat poured itself onto the floor, rubbed itself against her legs and purred loudly. She reached down and clasped it in her arms. The cat spent the rest of the night curled up on her pillow, occasionally stretching its claws into her tangled curls.

In the morning, the cat led the way downstairs to a large kitchen where the long pine table was piled with breakfast dishes, newspapers and a computer. Margot was emptying the dishwasher.

"You slept through the morning rush hour. Peter's gone to work and the kids had to catch an early bus. They're doing courses in the holidays. Nic's the musician and Rob's in an advanced French group. They'll be back around five."

Denise sat at the table and the cat leapt into her lap.

"She's called Jade because of her green eyes. Nic named her. Peter said it was a totally unsuitable name for a black cat and we all told him that cats are colour-blind, so what does it matter?" Margot explained. "She likes you. Don't get too fond of her, though. She's fickle."

Denise kept on stroking the cat.

"Did you sleep well? You were warm enough, I hope. I put an extra blanket in the cupboard, just in case. What can I get you for breakfast? I'm going to work from home today. The rain's cleared up, and if you want to go for a walk, I'll come with you. Tea?"

"Yes, please. No sugar."

Margot made tea and Denise sat in silence, watching. She delivered the large mug to Denise, who took a gulp of the brown liquid. "I've got butterflies in my stomach," Denise said. "And I feel sick."

"I don't know if this helps but my parents separated when I was about your age. I'm the youngest and my older sisters were already at university. My father went off with another woman and for a few years we didn't even know where he was. My mother was suicidal. No one was there to help me – at least, that's how I felt." She stopped talking. "Can I give you a hug, Denise? I don't know why on earth I'm telling you my miserable story."

"Now Oma isn't here any more, that's exactly how I feel… that there's nobody for me." Denise suddenly gave a sob. She wasn't sure if it was all right to tell Margot but she couldn't keep it bottled up. "The terrible thing is that I'm really mad at Oma for doing this. I'm so angry. I mean… it wasn't her fault that she got ill and died, was it? But that's how it feels to me. Like she went and left me behind."

Margot reached out and squeezed Denise's freckled hand. "Is it like your mind isn't ready to take in what is happening?"

Denise nodded. "What can I do?"

"Be gentle with yourself, Denise."

TWELVE

Robert was about the same age as Denise. He was tall, like his father and had a small gold sleeper in one pierced ear. He kept tossing his shoulder-length, slightly greasy hair out of his eyes. He had kicked her under the table when they were having supper. She had kicked him back and they had grinned at each other. She would have loved to have a brother like him instead of Felix, who was a wimp and a mummy's boy. Nicole was two years younger than her brother. She was thin and her eyes were like her mother's. She seemed shy. Apart from telling Denise that she loved her curly red hair, they had not yet talked to each other.

After supper Peter asked everyone to come into the living room. Robert whispered to Denise, "Dad and Nic have been rehearsing a tribute to Oma. My sister wants to study music and has the gross idea that she's a genius. Musical landmarks are one of Dad's things. It'll be OK. I'll make sure that the heavy part is short."

The large living room was lined with bookcases. Subdued lighting came from two reading lamps. A memorial candle burned on a small occasional table. They pulled the large, soft cushions that were scattered on the sofas onto the floor and sat cross-legged. Denise wondered what was going to happen. Softly and slowly, beautiful music floated over her. Nicole and her father played the *Adagio* of Mozart's *Clarinet Concerto*, she on her flute and he on the clarinet.

"One of your grandmother's favourite pieces," Peter said quietly. The five of them then stood silently in a circle around the memorial candle, holding hands. Peter and Robert said *Kaddish*, the mourner's prayer. Denise sobbed. Her two cousins put their arms round her. The tears flowed and a little of the aching loneliness ebbed.

Peter announced, "Blackstone Edge tomorrow. Got to show Denise why we live here. Who's coming with?"

Nicole moaned. "It's going to rain. I'm sure she's got better things to do."

"What's Blackstone Edge?" Denise asked.

"Stretch your legs and see a bit of the Pennines. Set out after breakfast, and get back in the afternoon. You like walking, don't you, Denise? It's about nine miles." Peter shut the door before she could answer.

"That's the way Dad does things. You don't have to go with him. He won't mind. And if you do, he won't talk much. Oor da's got nowt to say," Robert said in a broad Yorkshire accent.

Denise enjoyed the wind messing her hair and blowing across her face. When the rain started, she closed her eyes and turned her face to the sky and the heavy drops ran down her cheeks. Her legs seemed to take over and she began to run with a steady stride. She splashed through pools and jumped over mud. Her socks got wet and her feet squelched in her shoes. She jumped across big boulders.

The rain stopped and she waited for Peter to catch up. "Great views from up here," he said as he poured hot soup from a thermos.

"I love it here, Uncle Peter."

She left him behind again and ran so fast down the Roman Road that she could hardly breathe.

That evening Peter brought her a pile of maps and booklets; walks in the Pennines and the Yorkshire Dales and so on.

"Plenty of places to stretch your legs and blow away the cobwebs in this part of the world, Denise. By the way, Rob has nicknamed you Denby. Are you all right with that?"

She nodded.

"It's a compliment. Denby stoneware is a kind of pottery. It's almost impossible to break."

"Makes me feel even more at home in the north."

"Do you do much running, Denise? You've got a natural rhythm," Peter remarked.

"I did a lot of athletics at my old school. I'm quite good," she answered.

"Great thing to do," he said. "No one talks to you while you're puffing along. Oh, another thing. The brochure of Rylands School is on your bed. There's a place for you there, if that's what you want."

She shook her head in disbelief.

THIRTEEN

"How're you getting on with all of them?" Graham asked her, staring firmly ahead at the motorway.

"They're a lot of fun. It was mean of you and Stephanie not to let me stay with them in school holidays when I was a kid."

"Your cousins are about the same age as you aren't they," he commented.

"Robert is a few months younger than me and Nic is two years younger than him," she said. "And it's great getting to know them at last."

Graham sighed. "We didn't see the point of encouraging you to get close to them. They have different values from us and we thought it would confuse you."

She gave a dry laugh. "What you're trying not to say is that Auntie Margot isn't Jewish and they don't keep a kosher home."

Graham did not answer.

"But, Dad," she was angry, "they're my cousins. There's something special about being with them. And Peter's my uncle, and there are photos of him and my mother when they were growing up." She paused for breath. "How could you, Dad?"

Graham seemed not to hear her. She went on. "I don't get it. Years ago, you and Uncle Peter probably had an argument. You didn't have to take it out on me."

They were in the fast lane on a busy motorway. Graham concentrated on driving, pursing his lips.

"You've packed everything you need? Did they give you a list?"

"Oh, Dad, don't be a creep. I'm on my way to boarding school. I've left North London for good. This is a new part of my life and I want to be excited."

Denise looked at her father. He looked miserable. *That witch controls him completely and she doesn't even look after him properly. He looks like a homeless*, she thought.

"I'm sorry I yelled at you, Dad." He glanced at her. His expression did not change. "I'll miss you but I won't miss Stephanie and Felix. I'll miss my friends from school and my boyfriend. You didn't know I had a boyfriend, did you?"

There was silence in the car.

"Dad, did you hear what I said?"

He did not answer her for a moment. He was gripping the steering wheel and breathing hard. "Denny, you're the most precious thing I possess."

"You don't own me," she said.

More silence. She could only guess what he was thinking. They were approaching the Lake District National Park.

She asked, "Have you been here before, Dad?"

"Your mother and I spent a week in a cottage near Ullswater. It rained most of the time." He gazed ahead and smiled in a way she had never seen before.

The school was a converted mansion, probably a cotton millionaire's, built on a hillside with grounds that swept to the shore of the lake. Separate modern buildings were almost hidden by trees. As they drove into the car park, Denise watched a small group of students in dinghies with an instructor.

"I'll be able to sail," she squealed.

They parked the car and walked into the spacious panelled hallway.

"We have an appointment with the principal," Graham told the smiling young woman with a ponytail who greeted them.

"He'll be along in a moment. You can wait here. Would you like something to drink? Tea? Coffee?"

"You can still change your mind," Graham muttered while they were waiting. "If you're not sure, you can always come home, you know that, don't you?"

"Don't hold your breath, Dad," she said in a controlled voice. "I'm not a little girl any more. It was time for me to leave the family. A sixth-form college. It's a great idea, don't you think so?"

"You don't belong here, Denny. Not in this school with all these rich, anti-Semitic English girls."

"You're so ridiculous. I'm English and so are you. Anyone who isn't Jewish is an anti-Semite to you. I'm not like that. I don't stop being Jewish because I go to a non-Jewish school."

"It's a step on a slippery slope," he snapped.

Mr Sullivan, the principal, arrived at that moment. Denise stood up and pushed her hair back. His voice was deep and rough, with a strong Scottish accent.

"Come along to my office. You'll have a chance to see round the school. But let's have a wee chat first to get to know each other."

He showed them into his office and pointed to a well-worn settee and armchairs set around the huge black iron fireplace. Denise felt welcomed. The room was so large that at first she did not notice his desk and the filing cabinets. Oil paintings of Highland views hung on the walls, and Denise imagined the rugged Mr Sullivan as the chief of a clan, staring beetle-browed across a glen.

He saw her looking at the paintings. "They're to remind me of home," he said with a smile, and his brown eyes twinkled. "Now, Mr Levisohn, I'd like to hear your views. Are you happy about your daughter coming here?"

Graham cleared his throat. Denise looked worried.

"She's made up her mind. We'll miss having her around. My wife and I weren't happy with the idea at first but as we talked about it, we realised it would be help her to be more independent."

Denise blurted, "You made the right decision, Dad."

Mr Sullivan, nodding at Graham, said, "I understand. One minute they're small children and the next they're asking for the car keys."

"Mr Sullivan, I need to ask my father to do something. Would you mind?"

"Go ahead."

"I want you to tell me to work hard and enjoy myself."

"I wish you a successful new start, Denny."

So look as if you mean it, Dad, she thought

Mr Sullivan continued, "I've spoken to the principal at your previous school. She had good things to say about you. I'm sure you'll settle in quickly and be happy here. Now maybe there are a few things you'd like to ask me?"

His voice thrilled her and she wanted him to talk to her again, so she quickly said, "Yes. I want to know if I'll be able to run in the mornings before school."

"There are a few students who run regularly, so you'll already be part of a group. If you keep to the tracks in the school grounds you can run on your own whenever you're free. If you want to run along the trails in the National Park, our safety rule is that you only go out in a group of at least four and that you let us know where you intend to go. Anything else?"

"My wife wanted me to ask about religious services." Graham looked at his shoes and then went on quickly. "We're a Jewish family, you see."

Mr Sullivan smiled. "Good to hear. I grew up in Glasgow with a lot of Jewish lads. The school is non-denominational and there are no compulsory religious services. We have students from overseas and from migrant backgrounds. Tolerance and learning about different cultures is part of our curriculum. Does that answer your question?"

Graham mumbled.

"There's always a vegetarian choice in the dining hall," Mr Sullivan smiled, "and obviously Denise can take time off to join her family for Jewish holidays."

FOURTEEN

Am I still asleep? she thought. *Any second, Felix is going to shout, "Where's my clean shirt, Mum?" And Stephanie will call up the stairs, "Look on your chair, Felix."*

She opened her eyes. It was still dark outside. Her roommates were asleep. It was too early to get up. "It's delicious to feel happy," she whispered to herself.

She dozed, and the alarm under her pillow woke her at six. She crept out of bed, glanced through the window at the sky and the lake, and then put on her running gear.

The track around the school grounds was just over two miles. At first, the path ran uphill and then bordered on pasture for about half a mile. A sheepdog barked as she ran by.

She returned, still breathless, to the room she shared with three other girls.

The first eruption occurred late one evening as the girls were preparing for bed.

Tamra, tiny, sharp-featured and permanently

frightened, finally emerged from the bathroom. A strong fragrance of hyacinth air freshener followed her.

Beatrice of the large teeth and loud voice shouted, "It's a shithouse, Tamra, not a Hindu temple. Incense is for temples, not for bathrooms."

Olivia, whose peaches-and-cream complexion and blonde hair were almost identical to Beatrice's, echoed, "Not a Hindu temple."

"What goes down must come up, mustn't it?" boomed Beatrice.

"Want a spatula to stick down your throat?" her sidekick added.

"Keep up the good work, O slender one, and your bum will shrink," Beatrice added.

"Shut up and leave her alone, you bitches. Can't you see she's sick?" Denise said.

Tamra squeaked and scuttled.

"So redheads do have short fuses," Beatrice said to Olivia. Turning to Denise, she snapped, "This is between the Indian princess and us. Keep out of it."

Tamra was on her bed, curling herself up like a dormouse.

"Come on, Tamra. We're going out," Denise ordered. Tamra opened her eyes wide and grabbed a jacket.

It was late and most of the students had put out the lights in their rooms. The house rules were unambiguous and the girls were supposed to be indoors.

"We're going to walk by the lake," Denise told the trembling girl. "It's a full moon."

They sat for a while in silence on a bench. Moonlight shimmered on the still lake.

"Thank you, Denise. But I want to go back," Tamra whispered.

The school doors were locked and they had to ring the bell. A prefect let them in.

The next morning they were called to a disciplinary meeting.

Tamra spoke in short squeaks. The member of staff in charge asked Denise what she had said.

Denise censored out the complaints of cruel teasing by roommates. "She said she was feeling homesick. I suggested that the two of us go for a walk. It was my fault. I didn't realise it was so late." She did not add, at least not aloud, *and the rules about not leaving the dormitories in the evenings are ridiculous.*

Tamra squeaked again, and this time her words were clear. "Denise sticks up for me."

One of the prefects responded, "I suggest that there's more to this than meets the eye. The other room-mates should also be questioned."

Beatrice and Olivia were transferred to a room in an adjacent building and there was a discussion about bullying at the weekly general meeting.

Near the end of the winter term, Mr Sullivan invited Denise and two Nigerian students to a meeting in his office.

"January 27th is International Holocaust Remembrance Day, and that will be soon after the beginning of next term. We've been discussing what we should do at the school to commemorate the day. I've asked you girls here because at this school we believe strongly in the value of tolerance. Each of you knows more about the memories and tragic history of your people than any of the staff, and I would value your ideas."

"That's hard, Mr Sullivan," one of the Nigerian girls said.

"We're not asking you to be experts. It happens that Denise is the only Jewish girl in the school at the moment. Remember that only a few generations ago, Jewish students weren't allowed to study in German schools, one of the early acts of a racist regime. An evil regime with an ideology based on racial prejudice."

One of the Nigerian girls said quietly, "My uncle was a child in Biafra and his parents died of starvation. I've always been embarrassed to ask him questions. If it was for International Holocaust Remembrance Day, he might agree to tell me a bit about what he went through."

"Can we think about it during the holidays, Mr Sullivan? I'm not sure that I want to be part of this," the second Nigerian girl said.

"That's fine, Adaku. Think about it for a few days. Ask your relatives, if you want to. Read what you want. Make your own personal decision and then enjoy the rest of your holiday. We'll meet again in the first week of term."

FIFTEEN

"We'd love you to stay with us during the Christmas holiday, Denise," Margot told her when she phoned. "But Peter and I think you should spend New Year and the first week in January in Hendon with your father and stepmother."

Her cousin Robert came to the phone. "Don't expect anything to do with religion in this house. Mum's from a French family of lapsed Catholics and Dad's a Jewish atheist. But Mum's roast goose in brandy will give you a spiritual experience you won't forget in a hurry."

Margot snatched back the phone. "Presents are easy. We all buy each other candied somethings so there are lots of goodies around during the dark, long winter days. And it's the time of year to restock the wine cellar, so you can buy us a decent bottle of wine. By the way, your room is already decorated."

The goose in brandy was more delicious than Denise could have imagined. They ate too much and slumped on the cushions in the living room. Peter chose a CD of Bach and Robert replaced it with The Beatles.

It snowed lightly on Boxing Day. Peter wanted to walk round the lake and Denise, well wrapped up, joined him.

"Uncle Peter, I have to ask you something."

"Go on."

"It's about my mother."

"What do you want to know, Denise?"

She hesitated, trying to find the right words. "I found out that… I'd always been told that…"

Peter walked briskly and she kept pace with him.

"You found out that she didn't die in a road accident on the M1," he said without looking at her. His breath steamed in the frosty air.

"Yes, I did, and I'm not going to tell you how I found out. I asked my dad but he fobbed me off and changed the subject. So I asked Oma and she told me that I shouldn't keep thinking about the past. I think she also fobbed me off. So I want to know the truth."

"There's quite a bit to say, Denby, and it's cold out here. Let's talk about it with Margot later this evening. We'll tell you whatever we can." He warmed himself by flinging his arms across his chest.

"She was in Jerusalem, wasn't she?"

Peter nodded.

Denise sat with Margot and Peter at the large pine table in the kitchen. Robert had gone to see friends, and music from Nicole's flute floated celestially from the living room.

"Gabriella came to Israel to visit Margot and me," Peter began.

"I didn't know you lived in Israel." Denise was surprised.

Margot answered, "I'd gone there as a volunteer. A lot of young people from Europe did then. I wanted to travel and this was a cheap way of seeing another country. We worked hard, made friends and had a lot of fun. I had no idea about the Holocaust or the modern state of Israel. I was on a kibbutz in the north of the country and that's where Peter and I met. He wanted to live in Israel for the rest of his life and I wanted to marry him so I asked him questions. He was English, so why was he living in Israel?"

Peter interrupted her. "It's one thing being a volunteer and knowing that you're going to leave. But it's a hard country to live in and I wanted Margot to know what she was getting into before we got married. I gave her a short course in Jewish history."

Margot took over. "Enough of that. Don't you want to know why your mother came to Israel?"

"Yes, I do. But now I want to know why you two left the country."

Peter said, "Let's leave that for another time. Your mother only intended to be in Israel for a week. Robert had just arrived in the world and you were seven months old. She left you with your father and your grandmother."

"Was that the first time she'd been there?"

Peter nodded. "She couldn't make it to our wedding so she came when Robert was born."

"But why did she go on her own? Why didn't she go with my father and me?"

76

"She was only going to be away for a week. It was difficult for her to be away from you, Denise," Margot added.

"I still don't understand. Didn't my father want to go with her?" Denise asked them.

Margot chewed her lip.

"What aren't you telling me?" Denise's voice was urgent.

Denise grabbed Margot's wrists and shook her arms. "You have to tell me."

Margot said slowly, "Your parents were having a lot of arguments, Denise. Big arguments."

"What about?"

"She told us the marriage wasn't working. It would only get worse if they stayed together. She'd made a mistake marrying your father and then having a baby."

Denise did not move.

"Before they married, your father was enthusiastic and supportive about your mother's career. But he became a different person when she was pregnant. He demanded that she give up her career and be a good housewife and mother. He said it was his responsibility to support his family. She accused him of breaking his promise to her and he said he couldn't remember that he'd made one. He wouldn't listen to her. He didn't respect her ideas. He didn't consider what she wanted in her life. She said he was crushing the life out of her. The arguments got worse and there were physical fights."

"My dad's got a bad temper."

"Your father wasn't violent but he certainly hit her at least once. You can't imagine how awful it must have been for both of them. They had fallen in love, they thought they had a wonderful life ahead but it fell to pieces."

"What made my dad change? Did she tell you?"

"Your mother thought it might have something to do with his family. His parents were peculiar people, she told me."

"He's never talked about them."

"Were my mum and dad going to divorce?"

"Your father would have made that very difficult. He loved her very much."

"He loves me but he's very possessive."

"They both loved you. It was such a difficult situation to be in."

Denise thought for a few minutes and then asked, "Was she planning to leave him and make a life for herself in Israel?"

Margot nodded. "She hoped it would be possible to join the kibbutz but she found out that they would not have accepted her as a single mother."

"Why not?"

"Kibbutz is a community and the members have the right to decide who can join. In the past, some single parents had turned out to be an economic burden."

"My poor mother. What was she going to do?"

"We'll never find out, will we?"

"I don't know what to think."

"It's all in the past. There's nothing for you to think about."

Denise said she was going to bed.

That night she lay awake until dawn.

SIXTEEN

The library, usually a bright, attractive space, became a sombre location for an exhibition entitled *Man's Inhumanity: Questions About Genocide*. Black fabric covered the display cases.

Denise sat at a large table on which she had displayed family photographs of her grandmother as a little girl that Peter had lent her. Labels and arrows marked the relatives who had been murdered in concentration camps. Peter had boxes of photos and letters that he had taken from his mother's flat. The librarian found well-illustrated books from Yad Vashem, the Holocaust memorial museum in Jerusalem.

A girl Denise didn't know sat at the table to talk to her. "I told my grandpa that the school was doing something for International Holocaust Remembrance Day. He was in the army, and he was one of the soldiers who liberated a concentration camp. He said he'd never forget it till the day he died. The Germans in the town nearby said they never knew what was going on but he didn't believe them. He said smoke must have poured out the chimneys where they burned the bodies all day and all night. What on earth did those Germans think was happening?"

Denise nodded.

"Your grandmother wasn't killed, was she?"

"No. She got to England when she was ten."

"How?"

"Look. It's all written here. The Germans let a number of children travel to England and she was one of them."

"All by herself?"

"Her parents put her on the train in Vienna and that was the last time she saw them."

"That's so terrible. She was a little girl."

"She made friends with another girl from Vienna and they remained friends for nearly seventy years."

"Makes you think differently about a lot of things," the girl said. "About how people have to speak up for what's right."

Beatrice approached. There were several girls around the table looking at the Yad Vashem photos. She announced, "I think we should put all those awful things behind us and move on."

"We should move on," Olivia, her echo, said. "I hate thinking about things like that. They make me scared."

A girl with whom Denise ran in the mornings said, "You can't close your eyes to the terrible things that people have done otherwise they'll do them again."

Beatrice said, "How do we know they really happened?"

The girl was annoyed. "Those things happened all right. The Germans wanted to get rid of all the Jews. If you didn't know that, you've got a lot to learn."

"Why didn't they just become Christians?" Beatrice asked.

"It wouldn't have made any difference. The Nazis killed people who had converted, or who had one parent who was Jewish," Denise answered.

Another girl joined them. "I'm Australian. My pop – I mean, my grandfather – was a prisoner of war in a Japanese camp. He was furious when I started to learn Japanese. He said they were barbarians, and when we asked him what he meant he told us to see some films and he gave us some books to read. I couldn't believe the cruelty. Denise, do you think that any of us could do those evil things?"

"I don't know," Denise said.

SEVENTEEN

In September 2004 Denise began her second and final year at Rylands School and started surfing through courses at various universities on the library computer. The school counsellor suggested that she consider a BSc in sports science. *That sounds like me*, Denise thought.

One afternoon when Denise and her friends went into the fish-and-chip shop in Windermere, the fishmonger dished out their chips and asked, "What's going on up there at the school?"

"What do you mean?" Anna asked him.

"Didn't you read the local rag? Here, take it. Article's on the front page."

They snatched the paper from his greasy hands. Denise read aloud and the other two peered over her shoulders. *Future of Rylands School Threatened* was the headline:

S. T. (name withheld) was a top student at Rylands, a private girls' school, until a month ago. Her parents revealed that she had phoned them and begged them to take her away from the school. "We knew that something bad had happened because she loved it there, from her first day in the junior school, five years ago." S. T. told her parents, who are English Pakistanis, that she and four friends had received anonymous notes tucked into their schoolbooks. The words were formed from letters cut from newspapers or magazines, and the messages were racist. Whites only. Go back to India. *Graffiti had appeared on the wall of one of the changing rooms:* England for the English.

Mr and Mrs T have spoken to Angus Sullivan, the principal of the school. He promises to investigate the matter. It is well known that Sullivan is proud of the international mix at Rylands and wants to enrol boys in the sixth-form college next year.

We also interviewed parents who oppose this plan, who have formed an action group. They are worried that educational standards will drop if boys are admitted to the school. They are also worried that resources are being diverted to students who are not native English speakers, to the detriment of others, and that bringing in boys will lower the standards.

Rylands School has achieved excellence in many areas, including local sailing regattas in the Lake District. Now it looks as if there will be a need for skilled navigators in the stormy waters ahead.

"Did you know anything about this?" Denise asked Tamra, her timid roommate.

"There was something in my French book," said Tamra, her eyes widening in fear. "I got a horrible drawing. Someone had drawn the British Isles, but they'd drawn it wrong. There was a boat sailing away on the Atlantic Ocean, full of stick figures with brown faces. At the top of the page, in large letters, was a banner: *Go home to where you belong.*

"I think we should talk to Mr Sullivan."

"Malicious notes have been placed in schoolbooks," Mr Sullivan told the students who had assembled in the school hall. "If some of you think this is a practical joke, please think again. What you have done is vindictive, distressing, and has led to students leaving the school. If there are students here whose minds are darkened by prejudice, then we in this school have failed to teach tolerance. None of us have rights based on skin colour, religion or gender. Whatever else you learn at this school, this lesson will be essential for your future lives as adults with sound values. Prejudice has caused untold tragedy throughout history. It will not be tolerated in our school.

"While we're gathered here, I'll take the opportunity to tell you that progress has been made in planning for the admission of boys from the beginning of the next school year."

Denise whispered to her blonde bombshell friend Anna, "Shame we're leaving."

Not long after, a tall, thin man with an outsize Adam's apple unexpectedly stood in Mr Sullivan's place on the platform at the weekly morning assembly. He took off his spectacles and rubbed his eyes, then replaced the spectacles. "My name is Mr Perry Fordyce, and I am the chairman of the board of governors of Rylands School. The board works hard for the good of the school. But we do this behind the scenes, of course."

He nodded as he spoke, as if he agreed with his own words.

"Rylands is a splendid institution that for seventy years has educated generations of girls in these beautiful surroundings. With the utmost regret we have come to realise that certain ideas, appropriate and indeed excellent for other schools as they may be, threaten the future of Rylands if they are implemented without extremely careful preparation. Girls, I do not exaggerate when I tell you that the future of the school may be at stake if action is taken hastily.

"A crisis has arisen and, without going into the tedious details, I am pleased to announce that we are now on the right path. Mr Sullivan has agreed to cooperate with us in this matter. He will take a leave of absence until the end of the school year. The deputy principal, Miss Hammond, will take his place. Our hard work will continue. There will be minor changes in the school curriculum, but these should not affect many of you.

"Let me finish by wishing all of us success."

Denise strolled with Anna and Tamra by the lakeshore.

"I'll be so pleased to leave," Tamra said.

"What's going on? I don't understand. I don't believe Mr Sullivan wanted to leave. I've never met anyone as passionate about teaching values as him," Denise said to Anna.

"It's a takeover. Quite simple. Follow the money, that's what my father says. Where does the money come from? School fees. There's been a fight in the boardroom, that's my guess. It's economics for them. The commercial value of the school, that's what's important to Mr Perry Fordyce and his gang. We'll never know but my guess is that some wealthy parents don't like Mr Sullivan's values."

"But what about us, Anna? What will it be like for us until the end of the school year?" Denise asked.

"We just need to bury our heads in our books and make sure we get the best A Levels we can. They're too powerful for us."

EIGHTEEN

"Exciting times, Denby. No more school. Ever." Robert hugged Denise as she came into the Littleborough house.

"I'll dump my bags and join you in a sec." She hauled her suitcase to her room. When she tipped the contents of her school bag onto her bed, she noticed a white envelope with her name in block capitals. *My school report?* she thought. She opened it. The A4 sheet of paper that she unfolded had a large swastika drawn crudely in the centre. She threw herself face down onto her bed.

"What kind of people are they?" She began to shake with sobs.

Someone tapped on the door of her room.

"Leave me alone," she yelled.

The door opened and there was Margot with her arms outstretched. She sat on the bed, said nothing and stroked Denise's back. Denise sniffed back her tears and half expected to hear Oma's voice.

"How could they?" she sobbed. "Look." The swastika was on the floor. "This was in my school bag. Someone has been into my bag and left this filthy thing."

Margot bent over and kissed her. "Denby, darling, it's finished. You've left school. You won't see those low-life bitches ever again."

Denise straightened up and sat next to Margot on the edge of the bed.

"No, it's not over. There has to be something I can do. They took over the school and they're determined to ruin it. Margot, I can't just let it go. When they were so horrible to the Indian and Pakistani girls, including one of my best friends, I hated it. Now it's happened to me and I'm boiling."

"Of course you are."

"When I started at the school, it was amazing. At first I couldn't work out why it was so wonderful, and then I realised that I felt I belonged there. Everyone, whether they were a student or staff, was made to feel part of the school community. Do you understand?"

Margot nodded.

"It's what I'd always wanted, only I hadn't understood properly before. In London, I had this feeling that I didn't belong, that I wasn't a real member of my family." She sniffed. "When I got to Rylands, it was different. I loved being in the Lake District. The hills, the clean air, space to run. I know it sounds weird but sometimes I had the feeling that Oma was watching me and that she knew I was happy there. And I was happy, Margot. It was perfect, that first year. Everything was perfect." She paused. "Even though I had two crappy room-mates, but that got sorted out. Until they pushed out Mr Sullivan."

Peter walked into the room.

"Uncle Peter, why are there awful people? Why do they have to ruin everything? It always happens to me. My mother gets killed. My oma dies. The school where I'm really happy gets taken over by the hate crew."

Margot handed him the paper. He shook his head. "It never goes away, does it? The primitive hate. Who would have thought it could surface at a small private school with liberal ideas in the best setting in England?"

"Is there anything you can do, Peter?"

"Not sure. I've a good friend who's a journalist; I'll talk to him. Why don't you come downstairs? Being up here by yourself won't make you feel better."

"What are you going to do in the holidays? When are you going to London?" Margot asked Denise after supper while they were loading the dishwasher.

"I don't want to see my father," she said. "He'll grill me about school and then say he told me at the beginning I shouldn't have gone there. And I've thought a lot about what you told me about him and my mum. I don't even want to talk to him."

"I shouldn't have told you. He loves you, Denise. Don't make things worse for yourself. Has he ever shouted at you? Of course he has; what parent has never shouted at their child? But has he ever hit you?"

"No. He's never hit me, but he's never shown me that he loves me. He always takes Stephanie's side. He makes more of a fuss of Felix than he does of me."

"Maybe he finds it hard to show his feelings, and maybe you make it hard for him."

Denise laughed. "Whenever I can."

"Poor, unhappy Graham. He loves his daughter and she doesn't want to speak to him. He wants to know what you're going to do in the holidays and what's happened with your university applications, and you won't tell him."

"Stop it, Margot."

"Phone him and put him out of his misery. Decide when you'll see him and then tell him."

"I'll think about it."

When Denise was alone in the kitchen, she phoned her father.

"Dad, I'm coming to London for two days later in the holidays."

"Why not now? What's more important than your family?"

"I'm sailing with my friends for a bit. You know, to celebrate leaving school."

"You're doing what? You should be here with us, now… do I have to say that again?"

Let him roar a bit longer, she thought.

"I'll come when I'm ready and I'll stay only as long as I choose. OK?"

He shouted at her. "No, it's far from OK, but what can I do about it? I'm only your father."

NINETEEN

Inside the house, someone was playing a flute. Graham stamped his feet as he waited, and he had to ring the front doorbell twice before he heard footsteps. The woman who opened the door must be Margot. He hadn't seen her for years. Her dark eyes were like shiny jet. He watched the confusion spread over her face.

"Graham?" she announced in surprised and cool tones. "I'll call Peter. Come in."

The faint French accent was still there. She ushered him into a front room and turned on the lights. Bookshelves with bound copies of medical journals lined the walls and a desk covered with piles of papers stood in the middle of the room. There were two high-backed leather armchairs at the side of a fireplace. The room felt chilly, although it was a warm evening. Graham did not sit down.

His brother-in-law came in with a tray. There was a thermos of hot water, mugs, instant coffee and teabags. He pushed aside some papers on the desk and set it down.

"How was the drive?" Peter said. "Tea or coffee?"

"Where's my daughter?" Graham demanded.

"She's sailing with school friends in the Lake District. Please sit down, Graham."

Graham sat and watched Peter lower himself into the other chair and then stretch out his legs. *He's a cold man; everything is sorted out in his head*, Graham seethed.

"You knew that. Denise told you, didn't she? Why did you come, Graham?"

"She's my daughter. Why do you have to interfere?"

"Interfere?" Peter said, and looked at Graham, then tapped his fingertips.

"That's what I said. The word is perfectly clear. You just about abducted her after your mother's funeral. Now you keep her here as if you're her father."

Peter roared with laughter. "Abducted her? That's rich. She's eighteen years old, for God's sake."

Graham leant forward on the leather armchair and waved his right arm as if he wanted to strike Peter. "I don't want her to stay here in this house. She's got a good home in London. That's where she ought to be."

Peter said nothing.

"I've come to take her home with me."

"Don't be so ridiculous, Graham. She's not a child."

"Where is she?" Graham demanded. He pointed his index finger.

"Even if I knew, I wouldn't tell you. Those girls have had a tough year. They deserve their holiday."

"Listen, Peter, once she's back, you're to send her home and after that I don't want my daughter to have any more contact with you or your wife. Do you hear that? You've done enough damage."

Peter scratched his chin, stood up and poured cups of tea for both of them. Graham refused to take one. "I have no idea what you're talking about, Graham."

"I'll tell you what I'm talking about. I'll make it very clear to you. You're just like your mother who always thought that my daughter is part of your family and… besides…"

"Graham, you're talking nonsense. Denise is my dead sister's daughter. My late mother was her grandmother. That's family, isn't it?"

"I'm her father."

"Yes, Graham. And I'm her uncle."

"That doesn't give you any rights."

"She's an eighteen-year-old woman."

Graham grew pale and rubbed the back of his neck. "You used undue influence and coerced her to leave us. I want to tell you that I consulted a lawyer about suing you for abduction."

Peter threw his head back and laughed loudly. " Do you think we kept her in chains in the cellar for the last two years? She's always been free to go to you any time she wants. In fact, we've encouraged her to spend time with you."

"That's what you say, but you managed to tempt her to stay here where she doesn't belong, to keep her away from us."

"Graham, let's look at this from your daughter's point of view, as best we can. She wanted to go to that school. She wanted to be away from home. It's quite natural at that age. You'll agree with me that she flourished there, and now she's got a place at Exeter University. We can all be proud of her."

"You worked it all out, didn't you? You and your mother. You had it all planned. You hated the fact that I remarried and provided Denise with a mother. You did everything you could to undermine my wife."

Peter stood up and paced the room. "Graham, let go of the past. Denise has her own life to lead. You can't put her at the centre of yours. It's not fair to her or to you."

He sat down again opposite Graham and leaned forward. "You speak to Denise." he said. "She loves you. She tells you what she's doing and what she wants to do. Our children grow up and leave us."

Graham's jaw was clenched.

"Why did you come, Graham?"

"I expected her to be here." He shook his head and blew his nose into a tissue.

"She's found out, you know," Peter announced.

"What are you talking about?"

"She knows where Gabriella died."

"How did she find out?"

"I've got no idea. She wouldn't tell us. She suddenly asked one evening what her mother was doing in Jerusalem."

Graham covered his mouth with his hands.

"I had to tell her, Graham."

"You didn't *have* to."

"I told her that Margot and I met on a kibbutz. Her mother couldn't make it to our wedding and decided to make a short visit when we had our first child."

"I wish I knew how she found out."

"That won't make any difference now. I'm telling you so that you're not surprised if she asks you the same question."

Graham blew his nose again.

"I don't want her to go there. It's a dangerous country."

"Peter, she's strong-minded like her mother. She'll do whatever she wants and we all have to hope she keeps safe."

TWENTY

The large bed-sitting room in one of the student residences at Exeter University was Denise's retreat. On the second floor at treetop level, it overlooked parkland around the campus. There were bookshelves and a wide desk surface. Denise had arranged and rearranged the shelves; two rows of textbooks, one of romantic novels and detective mysteries. She put photos between her sports trophies. There was one of her parents gazing at their new baby daughter, and one of Uncle Peter and her mother as children, standing with their parents. She looked in second-hand shops for a few mugs and plates, a rug and an easy chair.

Her days began with her exercise routine. She ran for an hour, swam for three quarters of an hour and then went back to her room to make her own breakfast. She guessed that other students saw her as a loner, and there was truth in this.

Anna, one of her closest friends from Rylands School, came from Cambridge to spend the weekend in Devon.

"My latest man's family has a holiday home

somewhere near Torquay. He has a car, and I'm coming to see you."

They wandered round the campus.

"He's your *latest* man, Anna? You've been at Cambridge less than two months."

"That's why I chose maths. Lots of brainy, horny men. How are you in that department, Denny?"

"It's bleak. I'm not like you. I prefer one man at a time and there aren't any candidates at the moment."

"That's no good, my friend. What are you going to do about it?" Anna was a curvy blonde who exuded pheromones.

"I don't know. I don't feel right here. It's me, not the place. I feel nervous all the time. Like stage fright. It's like waiting for the starter's gun and not being ready to take off."

"That's not like you, Denise. Get out of your shell, girl. It's either evenings in the pub or trying your luck with the student societies. The guys are out there. You've got to find them. Isn't there a Jewish Society here?"

"I'm incognito," she said. "Maybe that's not the way to say it. The nationalist brigade at Rylands gave me a leaving present: a badly drawn swastika in my backpack."

"That's awful. Those last months at school were enough to shake anyone's self-confidence unless they were ten generations Anglo Saxon. But what do you mean, you're incognito?"

"I'm known as Denise Lewis. If anyone asks me about my religion, I'll tell him or her I'm an atheist. Being Jewish is a bit risky, I've decided."

Denise joined a group that regularly cycled the trails in the rugged landscape of Dartmoor Park. The men stuck together on the trails and in the pubs. She became friendly with a girl in the group who was a good photographer.

"This landscape's a real challenge. Are you interested in photography?"

Dartmoor was windy and bleak. The light changed quickly and unexpected squalls would sometimes drench the cyclists. Denise enjoyed the wild beauty and bought a digital camera. With characteristic persistence she took hundreds of photos to improve her technique, but her sense of loneliness persisted.

One bleak November evening there was a knock on the door of Denise's room. Pushing a stray lock of blond hair from his eyes, the tall stranger spoke. Would she lend him some sugar, please? Not waiting for an answer, he barged into her room and her life. His features were regular, his chin rugged. He could have walked off a film set. He checked her teabags, instant coffee and sugar, and slowly spooned some sugar into an empty jar, whistling softly. She was in her pyjamas. *Take the sugar and get out*, she wanted to say, but he had sat himself down in her easy chair.

"Sorry about barging in and all that, and hope it isn't too inconvenient," he went on, giving her no chance to reply. "Meant to get some sugar earlier but got caught up with a tutorial. Happens, doesn't it? Wow, did you take that photo of the old oak tree by the waterfall? What kind of camera do you have?"

He pulled out his wallet. "Keep a few of my favourite shots with me. Sun setting on Victorian brickwork. What do you think? Heard you were from the Manchester area. Love the Yorkshire Moors."

"I'm tired and I get up early, so I was going to bed," she snapped.

"Don't let me stop you." He smiled, showing his perfect teeth. *Lucky orthodontist*, she thought.

"You've got your sugar. Goodnight."

He stood up. Blue eyes, she noticed. "Wow, sorry for intruding. Just going. See you tomorrow. I'm Ed."

He strode out of the room, leaving her flustered. *The nerve*, she thought; *but who on earth is he?*

She saw him in the lobby the next morning. He walked alongside her, keeping pace with her even though she walked faster to shake him off. He was at the desk in the library when she checked out several books.

That evening, earlier than the previous day, he knocked again and barged in.

"Came to bring back the sugar," he announced, but he did not have anything in his hands.

"I would like you to leave, please," she said from between clenched teeth, and blushing.

"Whenever you say, but I would like to know a bit more about you first."

She opened the door. "Get out of my room." A few doors along the corridor opened slightly.

"I'm not going to rape you but if you feel safer with the door open, please leave it like that. Better to keep your voice down, though."

Denise was furious. "I'm asking you to leave. If you don't I'll report you."

He stood in the open doorway. "You're jumping to conclusions about me. Give me five minutes to make my case and if you still want me to leave, I will."

"Will you promise me?"

"Of course," he said, and paused. "The point is that I am looking for the perfect partner for badminton mixed doubles. I'm highly competitive and you look like the best candidate around."

She sat on the beanbag and scowled at him.

"I've been watching you for weeks," he said. "You're obviously the most talented sportswoman in your year. I've seen you run, I've watched you at the pool and in the gym. I don't want to embarrass you but your body is a work of art, beautifully put together. There's a challenge, though."

She raised her eyebrows.

"You send messages: *Keep Away. I Want to be Alone.*"

Her expression did not change.

"But you see, Denise the Disdainful, I think you and I would be an unbeatable partnership." She was about to protest. "Let me finish… to win the doubles badminton championship."

"Never played the game in my life," she said.

"Aha. Now you're talking to me." He smiled. "The basics are a piece of cake. You'll pick it up in no time. I'll book a court for tomorrow evening. I'm in second-year international studies, by the way."

"I'll play with you for two weeks and then I'll decide."

She was quick on her feet and her hand-eye coordination was accurate to the millisecond. After half an hour she was slamming or caressing the shuttlecock as if she had played for years. Ed explained the rules but rarely commented on her technique. It was fun even though her opinion of him did not improve. After each game, she would tell him that she was busy and rush back to her room. But the championship tempted her, and halfway through a particularly brisk game, she shouted out, "Let's win that cup."

He called her a 'firebrand' and a 'ginger panther'. He was fascinated by a freckle on her left cheek that was shaped like the Isle of Wight and he wanted to touch it. He walked closer to her than she wanted as they entered and left the court. She was careful not to smile when he made a joke.

She told Anna about him in emails. *He thinks he looks like a film star. He's right. I know he's interested, but am I?*

Two days later: *He 'accidentally' brushes my arm as often as he can. Used to hate it. Yesterday it gave me a thrill. What's happening?*

The first time she beat him at badminton, he sulked. She laughed at him. "You're too focused on winning, Ed."

"That's what life's about, woman." He stalked off.

Acting like a spoilt brat. Am not impressed, she wrote to Anna.

The next afternoon he came round with six red roses and apologised profusely for his 'immature outburst'. Could he take her out to dinner?

The meal was passable but the service was extremely slow. When the bill arrived, Ed complained to the manager, who apologised and offered them liqueurs on the house.

"You have to stand up for your rights. Otherwise people push you around."

She raised an eyebrow. "I can do that, Ed."

"I bet you've won a few shouting matches in your time." Ed touched her hand, and she did not pull back. "I like my women tough." *Arrogant bastard*, she thought.

As they walked back to the campus he put his arm round her. When they reached her room, he hovered.

"I'm standing up for my rights, Ed," she said when they reached her room, "and tonight I want to go to bed alone."

Before she went to bed, she typed to Anna: *If we win the championship, 'it' will happen.*

Denise and Ed were the clear favourites among the smattering of students who were badminton enthusiasts. They sliced their way through each round of the tournament and their victory in the final was a foregone conclusion. They went into Exeter that evening, bought a Chinese takeaway and sat near the river. Ed brought out a bottle of champagne from his rucksack.

"It wasn't such a challenge, was it?" he said as he shovelled noodles into his mouth.

"Ed," she began thoughtfully, "were you ever going to bring back the sugar you borrowed three months ago?"

"Why are you asking?"

"It would be an excuse to come to my room."

"Do I need an excuse, Den?"

"That depends."

"On what?"

"Let's go to my room and see how things develop, shall we?"

They sat on her bed and finished the champagne, passing the bottle between them. They wriggled closer together. "I feel a bit dizzy," she said as she lay back and pulled him on top of her.

A week later, they sat on some wide steps near the river. A small child scooted past along the footpath and her mother called to her to be careful. Three dignified swans glided upstream, ripples spreading in their wake. Ed ruffled Denise's hair.

"When did your family come here from Ireland?"

"I haven't got Irish blood," she said.

"Where's the red hair from?"

"There are family legends of a mysterious Scottish ancestor," she lied. *More likely to have been a Cossack rampaging and raping*, she thought.

"It's a relief you're not Irish. My father was in the army and was killed by the IRA in a bomb blast in Belfast."

"How old were you when it happened?" she asked.

"I was just eleven. I wanted to know all I could about him. He wasn't at home much, and when he was I was scared of him. My mum shut down completely after he was killed. The house became like a tomb."

"Do you have brothers and sisters?" she asked.

"One sister. She's not easy to get on with. She takes after my mother."

They watched a family of ducks swim past. Denise ran a finger along his spine and blew gently into his ear.

"Are you thinking about the army as a career?" she asked.

"Maybe. After my father was killed, I wanted to understand what the Irish problems were about. They go back centuries. There's passion and hatred on both sides. I still struggle with it. It's like my father's death had to be for something worthwhile." He turned to her. "Does what I'm saying make any sense to you?"

She nodded. "Go on. It helps me understand you."

He kissed her. "That's how I got interested in international relations. It's more likely that I'll join the diplomats at the jaw-jaw tables than sign up with the armed forces. My mother says I've got a way with words and I'd make a good diplomat. What do you think?"

"Mothers aren't always the best judges," she said.

"What does your mother think of you studying sport?"

The question startled her. Ed's interest in Denise had thus far been focused on the ways in which her presence helped him have more pleasure in his life. When on rare occasions he had asked her about her past, it was not from curiosity; it was because he wanted to regale her with some aspect of his own life. Their intimacy was limited to an almost telepathic understanding on the badminton court, and sexual gratification.

"My mother died when I was a baby," she said in a flat tone and looked across to the other side of the river.

He put his arm round her shoulder and said, "What happened to her?"

"She was killed in an accident on the M1," she lied.

"Did your father marry again?" he asked.

"I was brought up by a wicked stepmother, Ed."

"That explains why you don't trust people."

That's only a small part of the story, she thought, but said nothing.

TWENTY-ONE

One weekend in late May, she asked Ed about his plans for the summer holidays. They were lying on his bed, sticky with sweat from lovemaking.

"I want to be with you, Den, and do this most of the time."

She ran her fingers over his lips. "Perfect," she said. "We can do this anywhere, so why don't we think of a place we'd both enjoy?"

Ed said, "You'd like go mountaineering in Albania, cycling in the Pyrenees or sail across the Atlantic, Den. I like to be a lazy bum in the vacation."

She laughed. "Suits me. It's been a tough year and I've still got two big projects to hand in."

She was quiet for a moment, and then said, "What I'd like is to spend time relaxing on a boat trip down a river, lingering over good food and then going to bed with you." She ran her fingers lightly along his groin.

"What about the chateaux of the Loire?" he suggested.

"Sounds wonderful. My aunt's French."

The first two days, the weather was unpleasantly wet and cold. They stayed in the cabin on the boat, ate, drank wine and smoked pot. The third day was perfect. They set out on a long and leisurely cycle tour, taking a picnic and their cameras with them. It had been a enjoyable day. They were tired as they cycled slowly towards the moored boat.

Then Ed suddenly jumped off his bike and whispered loudly, "Hide behind the hedge, Denny."

She peeped through the branches and saw two women walking slowly along the towpath. They were walking with purpose, and peered through the portholes of the boats. The older one had to be English. Steel-grey, tightly curled hair, a crisp striped shirt and navy slacks. She was thin and angular. The younger woman would be her daughter, Denise guessed. She was about her mother's height and trailed half a step behind.

The women had found what they were looking for and were now waiting by the boat.

"Shit," exclaimed Ed, "my mother and my sister. What the hell are they doing here? How did they find out where I am? They were supposed to be on the Italian Riviera."

"We can't stay here all night, Ed. What are we going to do?"

"We could cycle back to the village and stay overnight in the hotel," he suggested.

"Good idea," Denise agreed.

At that moment, the younger woman called out, "Edward, Edward. You're there behind the hedge."

"My sister Sandra," he hissed, and slowly wheeled his bike towards the women.

"You're not on your own. I saw that you were with someone," Sandra said. "Can't we meet her?"

"Hello," Ed said, standing with feet astride. "Aren't you both supposed to be in Italy? Why are you stalking me?"

His mother looked down her nose at him and said, "That's no way to greet us. I thought you'd be pleased. You didn't tell me that you were going away with a woman."

"I don't remember telling you that I was going to be in the Loire Valley either, Mother. How did you find me?"

His mother sniffed. "That wasn't difficult. We have no intention of spoiling your little dalliance. I had assumed from what you told me that you would be with a group of friends. But no doubt that is what I was meant to believe."

"Holmes and Watson couldn't have done better," Ed said cynically.

His mother pointed at the hedge. "Aren't you going to introduce us to your friend, Edward?"

He hesitated and glanced over his shoulder. Denise emerged. "My friend, Denise Lewis. My mother and my sister."

"The trip to Italy didn't work out this year. Since we've run into you in this extraordinary way, Edward, would you join us for dinner this evening?"

"Denise, aren't we invited for dinner this evening?"

Good for you, Ed, she thought. "Yes, we're meeting some friends from university. We fixed it up ages ago."

"Then it will have to be tomorrow evening," his mother decreed.

"Are we free, Denise?" he said in a pleading voice.

"Thank you, that's kind of you," Denise said to Ed's mother, who looked at her from top to toe.

"Where's the red hair from? You're not Irish, are you?"

"Mother." Ed was abrupt. "That's not polite."

"I like to know where I stand with people. As you know, I have no time at all for the Irish."

And probably not for the Jews either, Denise thought.

The following evening, in an elegant dining room where French royalty would have been entertained several centuries previously, they were served pheasant with white asparagus, followed by a green salad. The goat Brie was perfectly ripe. Denise savoured every mouthful. The waiter, who had problems understanding their order, was from Eastern Europe.

Ed's mother, who sat as if there was a rod in her back, picked at her food and said to Denise, "Too oily and rich, don't you agree? The French are ridiculously vain about their food."

"I enjoy French food," Denise replied, thinking fondly of Margot's *canard à l'orange*.

"We prefer Italian food, don't we, Sandra?" Ed's mother addressed his sister, who was spooning the rum from a rum baba, clearly anxious not to miss a drop.

Denise drank more wine than usual and said little.

The mother leaned towards her and explained, "We go each year to the Italian Riviera and have been going there for at least ten years. This year, we were disappointed when our regular hotel was full. Do you know that part of Italy, Denise? Beautiful there; blue Mediterranean, perfect beaches. Edward had mentioned that he was coming to this part of France. I've never been here, which is not too surprising since I'm not fond of either France or the French. Our travel agent found us an extremely good deal and I decided that before I get too old, I should have a little adventure in my life. I have to admit that staying in a chateau is special."

Denise nodded politely. She was pleasantly and lightly drunk.

"Next year, back to Italy. One has to book early these days. It's getting so popular. The French Riviera has priced itself out of the market. The only people who can afford it are the Jews."

Denise picked up a bowl of crème fraiche and sniffed it. "Did you have some of this with the berries? I think it may be rancid."

TWENTY-TWO

One October evening at the beginning of their third year, Ed suggested that the two of them attend a lecture by a delegate from the UN. Denise was less than enthusiastic.

"I can promise you an entertaining evening," he said. "The title is *The United Nations: A Promise Unfulfilled?*"

"Sounds boring to me."

"Not a bit. There'll be a crowd, banners, shouting and maybe even a punch-up."

"Doesn't interest me."

"You'll be missing out on a bit of student life you haven't seen yet."

"What are you saying?"

"The focus is on the Middle East. The Jewish Society intends to show up. At the last count, there were six of them. They say they're fed up with the way the Arab lobby twists the UN."

"Sorry to be stupid but I don't see why it should be interesting."

"The Jewish Society is a joke. They're no more than a handful of students but they're like a red rag to a bull to the Arabs and the loony left who will charge at them yelling something about Palestine."

"I don't like the sound of it."

"You'll be safe. Our wonderful police will be around to make sure things don't get too rough. It's always a surprise to me to see how intense these people are."

He had grabbed her hand and was already pulling her towards the auditorium. She hung back, but he was stronger than she was.

Outside the hall there were two rows of students holding banners on which were written *Death to America* and *Death to the Zionist Entity*. Several were held up by women wearing hijabs.

Denise noticed a Kenyan student from her year, a brilliant long-distance runner. The previous week, they had worked together on a project and Denise had thought about developing the friendship. The girl waved to her.

"Come and join us. You can hold this banner."

Denise shook her head. "Just want to see what's going on," she said. "I thought tonight was a lecture about the UN?" She started to walk into the hall, but the girl caught hold of her.

"You have to understand. This is serious, Denise. Israel is a colonialist power that has no right to exist. It became a state because of a Jewish and American plot. It's part of a Jewish conspiracy to take over the world. Those are the facts. We can change them. You're either with us or against us. So if you don't join us you're with the Zionists who suppress human rights. Decide right now."

Denise had misjudged her completely. "Hey, we're students, remember. I'm here to learn, not to be shouted at."

"What's there to learn? Israelis are the modern Nazis."

Denise moved towards Ed. "Did you hear that? What's going on here?"

"There's something about Jews that sets people's teeth on edge," Ed said. "Haven't you noticed?" She shuddered. "I told you it would relieve the usual boring routine."

"Ed, I don't know much about the UN or what's going on in the Middle East." *But I probably know a lot more than you,* she thought. "There's always just been a war, or just going to be one. There's something I don't like going on right here, and I want to leave. Stay here on your own."

"Of course I'm staying. And you should too. This is international studies in the flesh."

He pulled her into the hall. It was crowded and they had to stand at the back. Students at the sides of the hall were waving green, white, black and red Palestinian flags. The UN representative was introduced. He managed three or four sentences before he was interrupted by a few students chanting, "Palestine. Palestine." Others joined in. The moderator called for silence but his voice was drowned out. More members of the audience stood up and joined in. The speaker sat down while the moderator held up his hand and again called for silence into the microphone.

Denise looked for the nearest door. She wanted to get out of the hall.

"Let's get out of here," she said into Ed's ear.

His response was to pull her closer to him. "I'll take care of you. Don't worry," he mouthed.

For a moment, the chanting died down. Then, from the front of the hall, a few voices began to shout, "Pal-est-ine. Pal-est-ine."

The crowd renewed a loud chorus. "Death to Israel. Death to Israel." More people were pushing their way into the packed hall. Denise and Ed were jammed in amongst the crowd. Tomatoes and eggs were thrown, and the speaker rushed off the platform. People began to push in different directions. The moderator spoke into the microphone but no one took any notice. A police officer stood on the platform and called for calm through a loudspeaker. The shoving and pushing eased as the hall began to empty. Denise was separated from Ed.

"What happened?" she asked two students as they walked out of the hall.

"It's a demonstration of the death of free speech," one of them told her.

"If you'd had your land stolen, you'd be want to be heard, wouldn't you?" the other one replied aggressively.

"This was supposed to be a lecture followed by questions. There are ways of making a point, mate."

Four or five other students gathered round them.

"The Palestinians have had enough. They've been massacred, expelled and stuffed into concentration camps," one yelled.

Another shouted back, "Where do you get your disinformation from? The UN declared that Israel was one of the nations. The Arabs started a war that they lost. And they still keep doing everything they can to wipe Israel off the map."

The student who was yelling the loudest shouted, "Hey, you dirty Jew. Go back to Germany."

Denise was horrified. Someone who was so full of hate could be violent and throw a bomb. She needed space and quiet.

Denise walked away quickly. Ed was with a group of students outside the hall. They were arguing loudly. Trampled banners littered the lawn.

He came over and gripped her arm. "Was that exciting enough for you?" He wanted to stay and to keep arguing.

"Ed, it was nearly a riot. A group of rowdy students who drowned out a lecturer and threw eggs and tomatoes. That's not my idea of fun. I'd rather have gone for a run. I need to get away from here."

Ed put his arm round her. She pushed him away.

"You're taking it too seriously, Den. There's still time to get to the pub."

She began walking towards her room. "I'm going to my room. I don't want to talk about it any more."

He walked with her. "The problem with you, Den, is that you don't want to know about anything outside your own little world." *There's a lot I know about, Ed. You'd be surprised,* she thought.

"If tonight's thugs and troublemakers are anything to go by, I'd rather stick to what I like doing."

"You take it much too seriously," he responded.

"The crush of all those bodies and the yelling scared me. I wanted to get out and I couldn't move."

He tried to take her hand.

"Leave me alone, Ed."

"Let's go for a walk. You'll feel better."

She began to run away from him, but he chased after her.

"You're annoying me, Ed. I told you to leave me alone."

"Den, you're in one of your bad moods."

"Don't hang around me, then."

He pulled her to face him and tried to kiss her. She slapped his hand and walked away from him, and shuddered again.

Back in her room, she sat on the rug, wrapped in a blanket. The words 'expelled', 'massacred' and 'dirty Jew' echoed in her mind. What was it Uncle Peter had said when he saw the black swastika? *Primitive hate*, that was it.

She began to sob. "I don't understand why my mother went. I don't understand."

The next morning, she cycled to Dartmoor, and ran for three hours.

"Where were you? I've been looking for you all day." Ed came to her room as it was getting dark.

"There's something… I mean… I had to sort out… I don't know what's going on with me," she stammered.

He sat on the beanbag. "You look awful. You've got black rings under your eyes."

She stared at him. "I told you a lie."

He shrugged. "I've told a few lies in my life, too. So what?"

"My mother wasn't killed in a traffic accident. She was blown up by a terrorist bomb in Jerusalem."

"What's the big difference, Den? She's dead anyway."

"How dare you say that?" she screamed at him. "Don't you understand, you idiot? I was a just a baby."

Ed stared at her. "I'm sorry. I didn't mean to upset you."

She did not hear him and continued to shout, "She left me and went to a place filled with hate and terrorists. She got blown up and I didn't have a mother."

He ran his fingers through his hair. "Wait a minute. What was she doing in Jerusalem? Was she some kind of missionary?"

"No, Ed. She was Jewish and she went to Israel to work out how she could live there."

He looked at her with his head slightly on one side. "She was Jewish? So you're Jewish?"

She said nothing. He stood up.

"Why didn't you tell me?"

"What was there to tell?"

"You should have told me," he hissed. "I don't like being taken for a fool."

"You're telling me that you wouldn't have gone out with me if you'd known?"

"You're a deceitful, lying bitch. Like the rest of your race."

He walked out of the room.

TWENTY-THREE

Around seven, after a sleepless night, Denise packed a suitcase and pulled her bike into her room for safekeeping. It took until the late afternoon to arrive at Manchester. She phoned Peter from Piccadilly Station and then waited an hour and a half for him to finish at the infirmary.

"Don't want to talk about it," she announced as she clambered into the four-wheel drive.

"Please yourself," replied Peter, who played a CD of Mahler until they arrived at Littleborough.

Margot was working in the vegetable patch. "Denby. What's happened? Are you sick? Wait till I get these damn wellies off my feet. Are you hungry?"

"Don't want to talk, Margot. Maybe tomorrow."

She ran up to her room. Jade the cat slithered round the door. Denise swept her into her arms, stroked her and began to cry.

"Why am I crying, Jade? I'd had enough of him anyway. It was time to break up. It wasn't a relationship at all. It was all about Ed – mending his hurt feelings, boosting his confidence, letting him choose where we went and when." She sniffed. "I need to learn from you, Jade. You're a self-centred creature and look what you get out of it." The cat purred as she lay across Denise's knees and gazed at her through half-closed green eyes.

Late in the evening, she joined Peter and Margot, who were nibbling cheese and biscuits. Peter had opened a bottle of Cabernet Sauvignon.

"I've decided to quit," Denise announced.

"Drinking or university?" Peter asked.

She groaned. "Don't be daft, Uncle Peter."

"You can drop the 'uncle'. It makes me feel old."

"Peter and Margot. This is my announcement. I've decided to quit university."

Margot frowned and said, "Wouldn't it be better to get your degree first?"

"I have to find out why it was so important to my mum to go to Israel. I can't think of anything else. I've got to sort it out for myself."

"Of course it's important to you. But so is your university degree."

"Margot, don't talk to me like a social worker."

"Have you thought carefully about this? If you wait six months, you'll have a degree that will open doors for you around the world. You'll be able to travel to Israel and anywhere else you want," Peter stated.

"It's too urgent for me. I can't sleep. I can't concentrate. It's got to be now."

"Has something else happened? You've managed to sleep and concentrate for twenty-one years," Peter said.

Denise sniffed. "It's too complicated to explain."

"That could mean you broke up with your boyfriend," Margot said.

"It wasn't just that," Denise said defensively.

"Tell me why you chose to live there." She looked at Peter.

He answered, "I started reading and talking about modern Israel. A people and a language brought to life again… and after what happened in my family… You understand, don't you? It made sense for me to plan to spend my life there."

"But you were born in England, like me."

"Finding your identity is a complicated business. A bit like peeling of layers of an onion. Yes, I'm English and love this country. My mother came as a refugee and loved this country. I'm a Jewish atheist. I'm a loyal citizen of England and non-observant Jew. When I was young, moving to Israel was an answer to finding out who I was. I didn't have to give up my British citizenship. I'll love England wherever I live. But I wanted to express that part of me that is Jewish and I couldn't do that through religious observance. I found out as much as I could about Israel and the Middle East. The more I learned, the more convinced I was that it was the country where I wanted to live. "

"That explains why you've got all those books about the Middle East in the living room."

Peter nodded. "They're still interesting to read. Some authors were uncannily accurate in their predictions, as it's turning out."

"But you left Israel and came back here. Why?" she asked. "Tell me, Peter. I need to know."

Peter seemed to lose himself in his thoughts. "As you know, we lived on a kibbutz in the north, not far from the border with Lebanon." he began.

"As time went on, we got more and more upset with what the way the country was governed," Margot said.

"I don't understand." Denise said.

"Every big problem was solved by going to war."

"What do you mean?"

Margot and Peter looked at each other. Neither spoke. Finally, Margot broke the silence. "It's almost impossible to understand unless you're there and ask people about their experiences."

"What you're saying is that I should spend time there."

Margot answered, "Yes, but in your case, not right now. We've still got friends on the kibbutz. You could learn a lot from them."

Denise hated the thought of seeing Ed again but now she was calmer, she was beginning to think that her impulse to quit was misguided.

Peter banged on her door. "I'm driving to Haworth and then walking across Brontë country. Margot's not coming and I'd like company."

"I just want to stay here and think," Denise called through the closed door. But when she heard the front door slam, she ran to a window and yelled at him to wait.

Her uncle strode steadily. People had crossed these dales for centuries, on foot, on horseback, in carts and carriages. Peter had once told her that his sense of the past was so strong that if he were walking alone, he would hold imaginary conversations with literary ghosts. They walked in silence. The wind and the squelch of her boots on muddy paths calmed her. There were a lot of sheep, fast-moving cumulus clouds, an occasional falcon and no other walkers. Gradually the events of the previous week started to release their hold on her. Sometimes she sprinted for the pleasure of speed and then waited for Peter to catch up. He had brought ham sandwiches and a flask of coffee.

"Did you go for walks with your parents when you were a child, Peter?"

"Sometimes." He looked sad, she thought.

"I don't know what made me think of Oma. Do you think about her?"

"Often," he said, looking at a cloud. "Don't you?"

"Yes. She was easy to talk to, wasn't she?"

Denise liked talking to Peter. He did not say much, but what he said was usually interesting.

"I like Devon, but I've had it with being a university student."

They walked on and went through a stile. Peter stopped by a short section of an old stone wall. "Come over here, Denby. Look, there's lichen and moss. There's an entry to a burrow, maybe rabbits. There are other worlds, Denby. With our inflated sense of our human importance we lose perspective."

She nodded, although she was not sure what he was talking about. "Oma would have stood here with an easel and painted, wouldn't she?"

"No. She would have taken photos and gone home to choose the scene she'd paint."

They walked on.

"Oma showed me a lot of pictures of the countryside in Austria. She used to say, 'Beautiful country, terrible people.'"

"When we were kids, she promised Gabriella and me that one day she'd take us to Vienna and Salzburg."

"Did she?"

"No."

"Why not?"

"I think she couldn't bear to go back there."

Denise shivered. "Her parents were killed by the Nazis, weren't they, Peter?"

"And her little brother," he added. "Did you know that?"

She felt a lump in her throat. Oma's family had been like Stephanie's, with parents, cousins, aunts, uncles and grandparents. She already knew this, but being here with Peter suddenly brought it all into focus.

She broke into a run and waited for him about a mile ahead at a signpost.

"I've thought of someone who would be really good for you to talk to," Margot said to Denise when they got back to the house.

"I don't need to talk to anyone," Denise said. "I'll sort this out for myself."

"It's someone you'd enjoy seeing," Margot teased.

Denise sulked. "Margot, you're getting close to interfering. I want to think it through for myself."

Peter looked up. "I can guess who you're thinking of. Great idea if we can find him."

"Shut up, Peter. Our girl's made up her own mind. Can't you see?"

Denise looked from one to the other. "Stop playing around, you two. Just tell me who you're talking about."

Margot began to stack the dishes.

Denise snapped, "Now you've got me curious and you have to tell me."

"It just happens," said Margot, dragging out the words, "that I was on the phone to the school counsellor from Rylands last week about a problem family and we began to talk about a certain principal who left."

"Mr Sullivan." Denise cried. "I'd love to see him. But where is he?"

"It turns out that the counsellor knew where he was and gave me his phone number," Margot said.

Denise blushed. She felt a frisson of excitement at the possibility of seeing him again.

"Impressive work, Margot. Get a move on, Denby, the phone's in the hall."

"I can't… I mean… what would he think? Could you phone him for me, Peter?"

"Where is he, Margot?" Peter asked.

"He's on the island of Arran taking care of his parents' B&B."

"I don't know where that is. How long will it take to get there?" Denise said. "Can I go by myself?"

Peter shook his head. "It's in the Firth of Clyde. You could go by yourself, but Margot and I would love to visit Arran anyway, even at this time of year."

"Let's all go together, then. When can we go?"

Peter stood up. "Where's that phone number, Margot?"

He came back about ten minutes later.

"Angus and Ina Sullivan would love us to visit. Business is quiet at the moment. We're welcome any time and they'll be delighted if we stay overnight."

There were heavy showers as they drove north. Margot and Peter did not ask Denise any questions. They played tapes of folk music most of the way. Denise wrapped herself in a rug and watched the rain on the car window.

Angus Sullivan met them as they disembarked from the ferry at Brodick. "It's great to see you again, Denise. You must be Peter and Margot. The island's not large so I thought I'd drive you over to the west and we'll stretch our legs at Drumadoon Point. It'll give you an idea of the scenery, which is something special. If the rain holds off, we'll watch the sunset. Ina's got a meal ready for us later."

He pointed to the soft grey peaks on the right as they drove across the island. "I'm thinking about what you might like to do tomorrow. There are great walking trails into the hills. There's a fair amount of wildlife too. We've got some mountain bikes and you're more than welcome to borrow them."

"I'm happy with an easy stroll for an hour along a glen," said Margot. "Denise and Peter are the energetic ones."

The B&B was a whitewashed farmhouse near a bay. Ina Sullivan came out to meet them. She had pale blue eyes, fair hair and a serious expression. Heather-clad hills sloped down to the beach. The clouds had cleared and the view with the evening light on the water was perfect. Denise took photos.

"It's good of you to come. You're very welcome. I've got a huge pot of lamb stew on the stove and we'll never finish it by ourselves."

Over the meal, Angus told them that his parents were selling the hotel. They were finding it hard to manage now they were older.

"That business with the school came at the right time for me," he explained. "It suited us fine to move to the island for a while."

Denise asked Ina whether they planned go back to Rylands in the future. Ina was still angry.

"Angus is a born educator. You'll have seen that, Denise. That school was his dream. Those people on the board want to move the clock backwards. They'll not get away with what they did."

"What will you do?" Denise asked.

"We're Scots, so we'll fight back. Angus has some powerful and wealthy backers."

They moved to the living room where Angus poured malt whisky for everyone.

"So what's next for you, Denise?" he asked her.

"I'm not sure."

"I heard you went to Exeter. Good choice."

Margot coughed. "She's almost finished her degree and she wants to quit."

"All right, Margot, I can speak for myself," Denise said in an angry tone.

"What's the problem then, Denise?" Angus said.

"I haven't really found… I'm not sure that I made…"

Ina, who was sitting on the arm of Angus's armchair, looked at her. "Was it the university or was it something else?"

"My boyfriend turned out not to be so nice after all," Denise whispered.

Angus smiled across at her. "A smart lassie like you would never let a bully with his brains in his underpants mess up her life."

"I decided to quit and do something else with my life. After all, having a degree isn't so important, is it?"

"I'll not try to persuade you until I've heard what you've got to say."

"I've decided to travel," she said, and felt stupid.

"Any destinations in mind?" he asked.

"I'd like to go to Israel," she said, her heart beating fast.

"I spent a year there on a kibbutz in 1966," Angus said.

Denise was astonished. "Why?"

"I went to school in Glasgow and had a few Jewish friends. They told me that it was a cheap way of travelling. A lot of fun for a young man. Hard work, lots of girls, music and dope."

Margot nodded.

"Did you like Israel?"

"Lovely country. Small, but so is Scotland. I met some amazing people in that year and I kept asking them the same question: 'Why do you live in this dangerous place?' They all said that it was their home."

"I don't want to make it my home. I'm English."

"You need to keep an open mind when you travel. A lass like you, with your talents and a degree in sport, will find work in any place she visits. That's the way to get to know about a place."

"I hear what you say," Denise said.

Back in Littleborough a few days later, she and Margot were finishing breakfast, "I've been thinking. If I've got a degree, I can travel and it will be easier to get a job." Margot nodded. "So I've put off the visit to Israel until August."

Margot hugged her. "Good decision. We're still in touch with our friends on the kibbutz. There's someone else who would love to meet you if she's still alive. That's Oma's cousin, who used to live in Haifa. We've got her phone number somewhere. And I'm forgetting that your father's brother – Barry or Brian, I've forgotten his name – also lives somewhere in the country."

"My father's never mentioned him."

"When you decide to speak to him again, you could ask him,"

Jade the cat curled herself round Denise's legs. Margot poured some more coffee. Denise began to talk about Ed.

"It was awful, Margot. This guy was so arrogant. But that wasn't the worst bit. He dragged me to a lecture on the Middle East. There were all these students, some of them from my course. I thought they were decent people. They had banners and were screaming things like 'Death to the Zionist entity.'"

"They were a crowd of ignorant students worked up by the far left," Margot commented.

"And then it turned out that Ed was anti-Semitic too."

"Then you're better off without him."

Peter rushed into the kitchen. "I'll drink my coffee in the car. I'm running late."

"Denby has decided to finish her degree before she travels," Margot announced.

Peter gave her a hug, a rare gesture.

TWENTY-FOUR

"I'll come to your office, Dad. I don't want to come to the house." The main office of Graham's many-branched estate business was in a commercial building near Hendon Central Underground Station. Magazines and newspapers sat in neat piles on a long, low coffee table. A profusion of plastic greenery decorated a dark corner. The furniture was unchanged from Denise's last visit more than ten years previously.

Marjorie, Graham's secretary of many years, greeted her with a quick nod. *She's still wearing that grey cardigan*, Denise thought.

"Haven't seen you around for while, Denise. He's waiting for you. Go straight in. You want to leave that backpack out here?"

For two years, she had avoided spending time with her father. Each vacation she made excuses. She had phoned him every two weeks. Their conversations hardly varied.

She hated the pleading whine in his voice and the guilt that lingered in her chest after their conversations.

The last, two days previously, the conversation had been different.

"Dad, I got my degree."

"Denny, that's wonderful news. I'd like to take you out to celebrate."

"There won't be time. I'll be in London for a day and then I fly out to Israel."

"Why are you going to Israel?"

"I want to see some relatives."

"I'll see you before you go, won't I?"

"I'll come to your office. I don't want to come to the house."

Now she knocked on the frosted-glass pane of her father's office door. Graham stood up and went to greet her with a hug. She pecked his cheek. His hair was thinner than the last time she saw him and there was dandruff on the collar of his jacket. He had put on weight, she noticed, and looked older and tired. Nothing in the office had changed in the six years since she had been there, including the dim lighting.

"My graduate daughter. I've reserved a table at the best local restaurant." He cleared his throat and spoke as if he was crossing a river on slippery stepping-stones.

"Thank you, Dad, but I'm going on the night flight and I'll travel to the airport from here."

He pursed his lips and then said, "We'll celebrate when you come back. OK?"

She gave a non-committal nod.

"How are you, Dad? Keeping well?" She sat opposite him. He took his time to answer.

"I'm fine, Denny. I'm on my own at the moment. Stephanie and Felix have gone to Bournemouth to stay with her mother until the end of the month. The house is very quiet without them." He looked as if he was going to say more but instead he rubbed his hands together. The silence was broken by both of them speaking at once.

"What did you want to say, Dad?"

"I had been hoping you would come home with me and stay in your old room tonight."

"I'm sorry."

He took off his spectacles, laid them on the desk, rubbed his eyes and took his time to put them on again. "How long do you plan to be in Israel?" he said in a bitter tone that she ignored.

"I'm not sure."

"If you like what you see, are you planning to stay there for the rest of your life?" He made a noise, a partial snort.

He was angry and loosened his collar.

She looked straight into his bloodshot eyes. "Have you been to Israel, Dad?"

"Never," he said decisively. "And I have no intention of going."

She crossed her legs. "My mother went, didn't she?" She spoke with quiet deliberation and watched his breathing deepen. He cleared his throat.

"I'll ask Marjorie to make us coffee before she goes home." He leaned forward to press the intercom.

"I don't want coffee. I want an answer. I asked you if my mother went to Israel."

"You already know the answer. Did I ever tell you the definition of a Zionist, Denny?"

"I'm not sure what you're going to say."

"You're mother lived in a fool's paradise about that country. It was me who was the Zionist. Not her."

"How can you say that? We both know that she felt committed enough to travel there when I was a baby."

"Most Jews don't live there, do they?" he said. "This isn't the time or place for a discussion about the need for a Jewish homeland. We can talk about that over dinner when you come back."

I'm being pushed into a corner and I don't like it, she thought.

"I give big donations to support Israel. That's being a Zionist. I'm a major donor, but there's one thing I won't give if I can help it. And that's my daughter." His eyes shone with anger. "Where are you going to stay?"

"With some people Peter knows who live on a kibbutz in the north."

Graham turned pale and a muscle in his cheek twitched. "You've spent too much time with that family," he growled.

"I like it there. He's my uncle and they're my cousins."

"We've noticed how you've avoided coming home for three years."

"It's been two years, Dad, not three. You said 'we've noticed…' Who's the 'we'? Stephanie and you?"

"Stephanie has always been a mother to you."

"Don't go down that path again. My mother died in Jerusalem."

"I suppose it was your uncle who told you about your mother?" he said sharply.

"No. I found out for myself some years ago. I don't understand why you kept it as a secret." She was surprised by how calm she felt. *I'm the one in control at the moment, she was pleased with herself.* She watched him rub the back of his neck.

"This is the time to get things straight between us, Dad. I'm asking you to explain now why you lied to me."

He took off his spectacles again. "Does it matter any more, Denny?"

"It does to me. You lied to me and now there's a chance to tell me the truth. Dad, we don't know how to talk to each other. We never have. I grew up lonely and miserable while I lived in your house. I'm going away for a while. One of the things I want to do is to sort out how I feel about my family."

"Is that why you've come to see me now?" He spoke in the whining tone that she hated. "To tell me what an awful father I've been to you? Just because you've got a degree and you're twenty-one doesn't give you the right to speak to me like this."

He can't manage to tell me that he loves me and misses me, she realised.

She stared into his eyes. "What I'm trying to tell you, Dad, is that I want us to speak the truth to each other. I'm going to visit Jerusalem to see where my mother died."

He rubbed his eyes, replaced his spectacles and cleared his throat again. He looked out of the window as he spoke. "There was no need for her to make that trip. It was a very dangerous time. I follow the news. She didn't understand how tense the whole situation was there. I pleaded with her. I told her she could go when things settled down; we could go together when you were a bit older. You were a baby, Denny."

"But she didn't listen to you, did she? Why did she go, Dad?"

He breathed heavily. "You're like your mother. Once she'd decided something, no one could make her change her mind. Her brother married there and she couldn't go to the wedding. When they had their first baby, she said she wasn't going to miss another opportunity."

"Did she go only to see her brother and the new baby or did she want to see what the country was like?"

"Both. She'd grown up with no idea what life was really like there. She was brainwashed by spending time in a Zionist youth group. Your mother's death was a tragedy that didn't need to happen."

"Thanks for telling me, Dad." She leaned forward and touched his hand.

He looked at her and went on. "What is there to say about Israel? After what happened in Europe, we Jews must have our homeland. But that doesn't mean that every Jew has to pack their bag and live there. It's a long way from paradise. It's got a lot of sorting out to do. Look at the problems."

His voice became louder. "Full of immigrants from Arab countries, Russia, Ethiopia. It behaves as if it's Little America. It calls itself a democracy but about twenty per cent of the population are Arabs who don't know or care about democracy. It's surrounded by enemies who will do everything they can for as long as it takes to get rid of it.

"Do you have any idea how long I've wanted you to talk to me like this, Dad?"

Neither of them moved. There was noise from the traffic in the street below.

Marjorie spoke on the intercom. "If that's all, Mr Levisohn, I'm going now."

"Goodnight, Marjorie," he said.

"And now I've got a question for you."

"What is it?"

"Why were you such a difficult child, Denny? There were many times when you were deliberately nasty to Stephanie. She wanted to make a good home and she tried her best. I made excuses for you, but you upset her badly."

"I was a little girl. She was the adult. And you always took her side. I used to go to my room and cry."

He looked pained. "All right. It's finished, Denny. It's history. I don't want to talk about it any more."

The outer door slammed.

"Let me take you out for a meal, Denny. You have to eat."

Denise said, "There isn't time. Tell me, Dad – your brother lives in Israel, doesn't he?"

"If you're planning on visiting him, forget it. You haven't got anything in common with him."

"We've got you, haven't we?"

"He won't want to talk about me."

"I may not like him, but I'd like to meet him."

"I'll tell you about him another time."

"This is the right time, Dad. I've still got half an hour. You've never told me anything about your early life except that you grew up in the East End."

"There's no point in dwelling on the past."

"Graham Levisohn, you bottle things up and you'll make yourself ill. This is the best time possible. You set time aside for me. I'd much rather hear about how you grew up than sit in a restaurant and try to make small talk with you."

Graham hesitated, stared out of the window again and began. "I try not to remember what it was like when I was young. I wasn't happy. It wasn't a good home. My brother Barry went to Israel when he was about your age and since you've asked, I'll tell you about it. Barry is three years younger than me. We never got on well."

He sighed and chewed his lip. "Our parents had a small corner shop in the East End. The East End used to be full of Jewish families, but they moved away as soon as they made a bit of money. They moved because it was a slum. They lived in old tenement buildings. Dirty streets. You can't imagine what it was like. We lived above the shop in a dirty, dark flat. There were rats. I never understood why my parents stayed on. My mother said they couldn't give up the business. That was nonsense because it was failing. The Jews moved out. Pakistanis came and opened up their own grocery shops."

Graham looked past her and went on. "My father had a bad heart and my mother was overweight. She was a screamer. She had a miserable life, but some of

137

the misery was of her own making. The only person she didn't scream at was Barry."

Denise straightened herself on the chair.

"My father would go into the shop to get away from her. By the time I was twenty I was studying law at University College. I'd managed to get a grant from the local authority and I was on my way out of the East End. My mother hated me going to university. She said I had to help my father with the business.

"That summer, my father had another heart attack. He recovered but he was very weak. I thought about the whole situation very carefully. If I didn't do something, we would all be trapped there. The shop was run-down but it was on a corner and it was a good location. Someone with a bit of money might be willing to pay a decent price if it could be made more attractive. My brother was studying at a yeshiva. You know what that is."

"Of course I do."

"I was the only one who could do something. I thought I'd be able to take a year off from university, but later I found out that I'd lose my grant if I deferred. I decided to drop out. I spent months building up a business that was going to be sold instead of finishing my degree. It was complicated because there were various contracts that had to be negotiated and I was young and inexperienced. Anyway, to cut a long story short, I got a decent price for it. Better than I'd expected."

He seemed hardly aware of her. He kept loosening his collar.

"Is that when you thought of working as an estate agent?"

He turned to her and nodded. "I realised that I had a flair for it even if it wasn't what I wanted to do with my life."

"So there was some money, and what happened next?"

"There was enough for my parents to buy a small flat in a nice part of Ilford."

"Did they want to move?" Denise asked.

"They said they didn't but that's because they were scared. I knew it would be hard for them at first but I was sure it would work out for them because there was a large Jewish community and some of their old neighbours lived there."

He stopped talking.

"Please go on, Dad," she said.

"My brother finished at his yeshiva. I thought that he'd start looking for a job, but he didn't. The next thing was that my mother told me he would be going to live in Israel."

He was scratching his neck again.

"What was he going to do there?" she asked.

"That's the question, isn't it? His rabbi had told him he was a gifted Talmud scholar and that he should spend his life studying in a yeshiva in Israel. He was twenty.

"My mother said it was a sign from God. Suddenly she and my father had a bit of money and God wanted them to give it to Barry so he could lead a full religious life."

"That was so unfair to them and to you."

He looked at her, and his voice was loud. "My parents moved into a small council flat in a working-class neighbourhood. People are snobs, you know. Old friends forgot them. They were lonely and ill."

"And your brother? What about him? Did he just take the money?"

"He thought he was entitled to it. He and my parents thanked me for my efforts. I took a course and became an estate agent. Both my parents died about two years after they'd moved."

"I'm a dropout, Denny. Not like you. And not like your mother either." He smiled wistfully at her. "She was very smart."

She went round to his side of the desk and kissed his forehead. "Dad, thank you for telling me this. I don't have to like your brother, but I want to meet him. Where do you think he is now?"

"I know where he is."

"You've been in touch with him?"

"No. He lives near Hebron and his name came up in a news item about two months ago. I'd prefer that you don't travel out to any of those settlements. They're not safe."

"Do me a favour, Denny."

"What?"

"Listen, Denny, if you're determined to do this, go for two weeks and see what you think then. I'll pay for a good hotel and give you money so you can go on tours. Then come back to London and tell me what you think."

"It's too short. I want to give myself the option of staying longer if I like it there."

"I don't want us to part on bad terms. You're excited. This is something you've wanted to do for a long time. I can understand that but do this for me. You're travelling tonight. I haven't seen you for two years. When am I going to see my girl again?"

Emotional blackmail, she thought.

"I want you to come back after two weeks and tell me about it. I'm asking for us to have that celebration meal when you come back."

"I wanted to spend a year travelling, Dad. To be a backpacker. To spend as much time as I want in the places I visit."

"I'm not stopping you. I'm just asking you to delay it for two weeks. Is that too much to ask?"

Denise sighed. "I'm glad we can talk like this, Dad."

They looked at each other without speaking.

"Promise me that you'll come back after two weeks."

"It means I'll have to make different arrangements with my ticket and it'll cost a whole lot."

"I'll pay. You know I will."

"I promise. I have to leave for the airport now, Dad."

She stretched out her arms to him and they hugged.

"Take care of yourself, Denny."

PART THREE

ISRAEL

AUGUST TO DECEMBER 2008

TWENTY-FIVE

The café was still there. It was in a street crowded with old stone-clad buildings three and four storeys high, some with small wrought-iron balconies. The Jaffa Road in Jerusalem was a photographer's delight, familiar to Denise from pictures in Peter's books.

The name of the café had been changed. Four tables stood outside under white sunshades. There was no remembrance plaque of the terrorist attack.

As she opened the door, conversation-drowning music with a strong beat hit her and she wondered if it was now a bar. She was hot and thirsty. The backpack had started to weigh her down.

The place was nearly full. The tables were close to each other and she had to weave herself and her backpack through to a small table near the back. Two young women, their heads covered with floral headscarves, were at the table next to her. Their babies waved chubby fists at each other from their mothers' laps. A large black-and-white photo of the neighbouring shops and the café was probably some kind of memento. *No one in here except me*, Denise thought, *would know.*

A short, plump waitress with a pink streak in her black hair put a jug of water and a tumbler on the table.

"Do you have a menu in English?" Denise asked. She ordered orange juice and a sandwich and gulped down two glasses of water. The order arrived and she pushed it to one side. Since she was sixteen and had discovered how her mother died, she had waited for this moment. *Did my mother sit here? Was she looking out at the street? What did she see just before she died? Was that dress shop there at the time? What was she wearing?*

"My mother was killed here in the terrorist attack," she announced in English to the waitress who brought the bill.

The girl nodded and smiled. Denise guessed she either hadn't heard or hadn't understood.

Then she spotted a woman with wrinkles round her eyes and dyed red hair who leaned on her elbows by the cash register.

"My mother was killed here in the terrorist attack and I'd like to leave these flowers." She held out the five white roses she had bought from a street stall down the hill.

"That's terrible. What would you like me to do with the flowers?" The woman smiled, and Denise suddenly felt sad.

"I thought I'd leave them in the street by the door."

"In this heat? In five minutes they'll just dry up." The woman took the roses and fingered them lightly. "They're lovely. Would you like me to put them in a vase on the counter?"

"Wait. Have you got a piece of paper? I want to write my mother's name and explain that she was killed here. Could you tape that to the vase?"

"She was here in 1987?" the woman said when she read what Denise had written. "That was the Intifada; bombs on buses, in shops, in cafés. It was awful. Would you like me to write this in Hebrew too?"

"Thank you," Denise said quietly.

The bus station in Jerusalem was crowded, hot and noisy. There were soldiers with guns who looked about the same age as Denise's brother, Orthodox men and women with small children in strollers, girls in shorts and T-shirts, and backpackers like herself. Everyone except her knew where to go in a building where it was easier to buy ice cream than to find a sign in English to indicate where one bought a bus ticket.

Excitement had kept her awake throughout the night flight. On the darkened plane, other passengers had covered their eyes and slept. She fell asleep as soon as the bus from Jerusalem to Haifa started moving.

At the bus station in Haifa she asked an older woman. "Where's the bus to Nahariya?" At first she pointed vaguely but when she saw that Denise was confused she took her directly to the bus stop.

The bus to Nahariya was cool at first but the air conditioning broke down after fifteen minutes. People complained in a variety of languages and with much more noise than any she had heard on buses in England.

At a stop along the way a soldier got on the bus. Denise noticed his quick grin as he said something to another soldier who was already seated and slapped him on the shoulder. He sat down on the empty seat next to her and fell asleep straight away. His head lolled onto her shoulder. His gun, which he continued to clutch, pressed against her leg. His uniform was shabby, his boots dusty and he smelled of sweat. He hadn't shaved for a few days and his beard was ginger.

She was too hot to think and too tired to be interested in the scenery. She felt a strong urge to run her fingers through the soldier's black curls. He woke and said something that sounded like *mushabashka.*

"I don't speak Hebrew," she said.

"What's the time?" he demanded in the abrupt way most people had spoken to her at the bus stations in Tel Aviv and Haifa when she asked directions.

They don't apologise for anything here, she thought. *This soldier's dribbled on my arm and jammed his gun into my leg and he speaks to me as if I've done something wrong.* But he smiled at her again, so she liked him. He had blue eyes, and she wanted to touch the band of tiny freckles across his nose.

"I'm Kobi," he said. "What's your name?"

He started to laugh when she told him, and she laughed with him.

"Dennis? That's a man's name. You look like a girl."

"It's Denise, not Dennis. I am a girl. Can't you tell?"

"Your parents got confused, or maybe they wanted a boy?"

"Denise is a girl's name."

"You like your name?"

"Yes. I've always liked it."

"Denise. Denise." He rolled the name around as if he was tasting it. "I've never met a Denise. If you live in America it's a nice name, but it's not a Jewish name. Now you're in Israel. Your name will be Dina."

"I'm English, Kobi, and I'll decide what my name is." She was enjoying herself.

"Are you from London?"

She nodded.

"When did you arrive in Israel?"

"This morning," she said.

"So now I know all your story. Why you're here and what you are going to do. You have relatives in Nahariya. There is a *simcha*, a wedding, I think." He looked seriously again at her face as if trying to read her thoughts. "You've come to Israel before, when you were a child with your parents. This time you are going to travel around the country with your friends, but first you are going to Nahariya for the wedding. I am right? You see, Dina, I'm very smart. I look at you and I know everything. I'm right, yes?"

"You're wrong about everything, Kobi."

"OK. Now tell me why you're here."

"I'm going to visit a kibbutz. My uncle and aunt used to live there."

"Which kibbutz?"

When she told him, he squeezed her knee. "Hey, that's my kibbutz. Do your uncle and aunt still live there? What are their names?"

"They left years ago and went back to England."

"Is someone meeting you at the bus station?"

"Someone called Benjy."

"This is crazy. He's my *abba*. My dad. He's from London. My mum, she's Israeli. Me? I'm Israeli. I've been a soldier for a month and now I'm going home. I'm a reserve soldier. You know what that means?"

"I think so. You're not a regular soldier. Is that right?"

"Mm. You know about Israel?"

"This is the first time I've been here."

He touched her shoulder. "I have to show you around." He flicked her curls. "I like your hair. You have a terrible temper, yes?"

"And fire comes out of my nose when I'm angry. Watch out, Kobi."

Benjy was waiting at the bus station. He was a cube on short legs and wore dark blue work clothes. He had a round face and a fringe of black hair. Sweat ran down his face. He scratched his head as he saw the redhead chatting to his son.

"Abba." Kobi hugged him and gabbled in Hebrew, waving an arm. Then he switched to English. "This is your friend from London, Dina."

"I came to meet a girl called Denise," Benjy said.

"That's me. Your son didn't like my name so he gave me a new one."

Benjy nodded but didn't smile. "Hop in the back, Denise." He sounded like a London taxi driver. He cleared a space among the piles of clothes and packages that littered the back seat and Kobi climbed in next to his father. They ignored her and talked in Hebrew.

The ride was short and uncomfortable. Kobi disappeared as soon as Benjy parked the car, waving his hand and shouting, "*Lehit.*"

"I'll take you to our house," Benjy said. She wished he'd ask her about her journey or say something about Peter.

"This way," called Benjy as they crossed a well-watered lawn. "That's the dining room." He pointed to a warehouse-size building with a sculpture outside, walked quickly and turned along a path hedged with tall oleander shrubs. The small houses in rows looked identical: shaded front doors with windows on each side.

"Here's the house."

Denise noticed hanging baskets of pink and white impatiens and a nameplate on the door in English and Hebrew.

He switched on the air conditioning and the small living room filled with a rattling noise. "Yael is working until after lunch. I've got to get back to work, so come in and make yourself comfortable." He wiped his forehead. "You'll be sleeping on the couch."

Folded sheets and towels lay on the couch ready for her to use. Two worn easy chairs stood opposite. On the coffee table was a bowl of almonds. The room had a small dining area with two wooden chairs and a wooden table with a lace doily, on which there was a bowl of apples and pears. Next to the large fridge was a kitchenette with a sink, a hotplate and a microwave. The room was overfilled with furniture but it was neat, bright and clean.

She felt uncomfortable about imposing herself on people she did not know. Her brain felt like an overcooked cauliflower. It was too hot to think, talk or do anything. She showered. Cold rivulets ran over her face and body and gradually she began to feel human again. She wrapped the towel round herself and went into the sitting room.

In the fridge was a jug of cold lemonade. She poured herself a drink and looked around the room again. There were prints of Renoir and Monet. One of the bookshelves held books about art and artists; another, English paperback novels. A shelf unit on the wall above one of the easy chairs had a row of photos: Kobi in his uniform, Kobi with his parents, Benjy driving a tractor, and two women smiling at the camera. Cushions in primary colours were scattered on a sofa that was too big for the space. A small corner display cabinet with carved wooden flowers on the doors held Lladro porcelain figures of a harlequin and a shepherdess. She remembered that Oma had the same figurines on her mantelpiece.

She had not eaten since early morning and was feeling hungry. She dressed quickly. It was easy to find her way back to the dining room but once she entered the high-ceilinged hall with rows of mostly empty tables, she did not know what to do. A thin, harassed-looking woman who could have been between thirty and fifty and was not wearing a bra asked her if she was the new volunteer. "Where is she? She should have been on the bus." It seemed as if the woman expected Denise to know.

A scruffy young man with torn shorts told her to take whatever she wanted to eat from the trolleys and sit with him and his friends. He waved his arm to indicate four young people who had finished eating and were talking. "We're volunteers."

The salads looked tired and oily and there was some kind of grain that apparently was eaten with boiled vegetables. She took two slices of bread, cream cheese, some olives and a spoonful of two of the salads.

A blond guy pushed his long hair from his eyes and called out to her. "You the new volunteer?"

"No. I'm a guest of Benjy and Yael."

"You're supposed to tell someone that you're a guest for Shabbat so they know who you are. But they're fairly slack about security here."

"It is not so," said a German girl. "It is a small place and someone in charge knows about these things."

She was probably right, Denise thought, when a red-faced, sweating woman asked, "You are staying with Yael and Benjy, yes? Are you family?"

The house was quiet when she got back. She poured herself another glass of lemonade. As soon as she sat on the sofa, a small, wiry woman with a lot of wild hair rushed out of the bathroom. She had a bucket of water in one hand.

"I'm Yael. I need to wash the floor. Please sit outside for ten minutes."

Denise, who had been travelling for what seemed like a week, felt hurt by the abrupt remark.

After cleaning the floor, Yael took Denise's hand and pulled her back into the house.

"Everything is such a rush on Fridays. I never had good manners and I was rude to you. You must be tired. You had lunch?" Denise nodded. "Good. And Benjy was there to collect you?" She offered Denise almonds. "Welcome,

Denise. I want to hear about Peter and Margot. They are well? But now you're tired. Have a rest on our bed."

Yael pulled down the shutter to darken the room. Denise collapsed on the soft bed and fell asleep.

A loud argument in the living room woke her. A couple had joined them. Yael had pinned up her hair and wore an embroidered white blouse.

"My sister and brother-in-law, Timna and Maor," Yael explained. "They live near us."

Maor, the brother-in-law, was too tall for the armchair. He helped himself to a handful of almonds and asked Denise, "You understand Hebrew?"

Denise shook her head.

"I'll explain." He sounded like a military officer. "Denise, we wanted to show you straight away what is kibbutz life. If there is something to say, we say it very loudly. Everyone has the right to talk, but no one listens. Also, you have to understand that on kibbutz, everyone is equal but like the English writer says, some are more equal than others."

Timna was a tense, small woman with sharp features who looked like her sister. She wore a sleeveless dress with a floral pattern. Her arms were thin. She inspected Denise from top to toe. "We are going overseas tomorrow for two weeks. Our house is very near here. If you want, you can stay there and water the plants."

"Thank you," Denise said.

After the guests left, Yael told Denise that on Friday evenings dinner was served in the communal dining room. Denise changed into a white cheesecloth blouse and green Liberty print skirt.

The large hall was transformed from the institutional dining room in which she had eaten lunch. The tables were covered with white tablecloths. Each had a vase of flowers and a plaited challah. In one corner there was a table with sets of candlesticks.

"Most of the members here are not observant but some of us like to light candles on Shabbat. Do you want to join me?" Yael invited her.

"No thank you."

Candles on Friday evenings and blessings over the wine and bread flooded Denise with memories. She remembered her father blessing Felix and her. Before the meal, he would chant the *Kiddush*, which she thought of as a tuneful jabber of words. Halfway through he would always smile at her. Those were the few moments in her childhood when he showed her affection.

Before the meal was served, a young woman read a Hebrew poem. Three young men and a girl, all in white shirts, sang a song she didn't know accompanied by a guitar. The room was chilly from the air conditioning. *It's so familiar and so strange at the same time*, Denise thought.

Yael reached across the table and squeezed her hand. "Shabbat Shalom, Denise, your first Shabbat in Israel."

Chopped liver, salads, chicken soup, roast chicken and baked potatoes were served from trolleys. The meal was already halfway through when Kobi came into the dining room with two other young men. Yael saw Denise looking at the table where they sat and said, "He'll come to the house for a visit before he goes to the pub this evening. All the young people go to the pub on Friday evening. You'll go with him, yes?"

"It's lovely here," she said to Benjy when they were back at the house.

He leaned back in his armchair. "Except when it isn't."

She had labelled him as Grumpy, one of the seven dwarfs.

He looked at her intensely from under his bushy black eyebrows. "What brought you to Israel, Denise?"

She shifted in her chair and blushed. "I'm just interested. That's all."

Benjy pierced her with his gaze. "You don't like being asked questions, do you?"

"I don't mind."

"Tell me about yourself," Benjy demanded.

"How do I answer a question like that?"

"However you want, girlie."

Yael put some cake on the table and asked if she wanted iced coffee.

"Don't let him push you around, Denise. Benjy, she's only just arrived. Leave her alone."

"What if I told you that I've longed to come to Israel since I was a little girl?"

"I wouldn't buy it," Benjy said. "You're not like your mother. She was the dedicated Zionist type." *He makes up his mind about people quickly*, Denise thought.

Yael was annoyed. "Benjy, leave her alone. She's a young woman and she doesn't have to tell you anything." She turned to Denise. "Benjy is like a rhinoceros, that's the right name for the animal? He attacks people with his questions. But you can say what you want to him. His skin is tough. Don't let him upset you. You know we met your mother when she came to stay with Peter and Margot?"

Benjy charged on with his questions, leaning forward and peering at her. "You want to know why your mother came. Right?" His dark eyes glistened. He leaned back in the chair. *Rhinoceros*, Denise thought.

"I know that she came to visit Peter and Margot when their first child was born."

"That's not the whole story."

Yael cut in. "If there's something we can help you with, you must ask us. Kobi will be here soon. He'll take you to the pub. You don't want to spend the evening with us, I'm sure. I'll put sheets on the couch for you. You stay here only for tonight. In the morning, I take you to my sister's house, and there you will have the whole house to yourself."

Benjy suddenly broke into their conversation. "Peter and me, we were friends in London. I knew your mother too."

"How old are Peter and Margot's children now, Denise? The boy is about the same age as you. He's at university? Is he going to be a doctor like his father?"

"He's in France. At the University of Grenoble. He's studying French literature."

"Margot's French, isn't she? I'd forgotten."

"Benjy, why did Peter go back to England?"

"Didn't he explain? He said he couldn't see a future for this country unless there was a government that did everything possible to make a peace agreement. He said every government tried to solve problems and win elections through military conflict. We argued for hours. I said we had to defend this country."

Denise wished he would talk more about her uncle and less about the war and politics.

"I've thought a lot about what he said. We've had so many wars over the years. We can fight and we can win, but until we find the way to make peace, people like your Uncle Peter will keep leaving. It's a tragedy. The people who could give the most to this country are being driven away."

"My uncle told me that this is a tough country to live in."

"Peter said that he couldn't go on living here because if he had kids they might have to give their lives for something he'd stopped believing in. These days I think he was right and I was wrong. The early Zionists were building a dream. It's not going to happen. Israel will never be accepted as part of the Middle East."

"She's had enough, Benjy." Yael smiled at Denise. "He talks too much. I remember those arguments. Benjy would be shouting and making speeches. Peter would be quiet most of the time. But when he said something, it was always worth listening to." Her face softened when she smiled. "How long are you here for?"

"Two weeks," Denise said.

Benjy exploded. "Two weeks! You won't learn much about this country in two weeks. Go on some tours. Go to Jerusalem, the Dead Sea and Masada. Go to Eilat and snorkel. There's a lot to see. No point in staying on a small kibbutz way up north. Kibbutz is a bubble. We live in our own little world."

"I've come to meet a few relatives who live here. I haven't come to see if I want to spend the rest of my life here."

Benjy raised his eyebrows. "Where do your relatives live?"

"My grandmother had a cousin who lived, or lives, in Haifa. She always talked about her. I've got her phone number but it's a few years old."

"You can phone from here if you want."

"I don't want to impose, but—"

Benjy laughed. "You're such a polite English girl. Give yourself a break. You're in a different country; you've only just arrived. In Israel if you don't ask, you won't get."

Yael turned to Benjy. "She's our visitor. Do you know if your relatives are religious?"

"Why?"

"Because it is Friday evening, and if they are it would be best to wait until the Shabbat is finished tomorrow."

Denise knew a great deal about the rules of the Sabbath. The Friday afternoon routine of getting ready by switching on lights and hotplates so that they could live with the convenience of electricity for twenty-four hours without touching a switch; no television, and fights with Stephanie, who intruded into her room and found her wearing earphones and listening to music.

"I don't think they're religious. I don't really know. I'm sure it would be all right to phone this evening."

The door burst open. Kobi, shaved and wearing a T-shirt and jeans, crashed in. For Denise he was bathed in a soft glow.

"You came at the right moment," Yael said. "Your father's getting warmed up and our guest is getting bored."

Kobi hugged his mother and pecked his father's cheek. He stretched out his arms and pulled Denise off the sofa.

"I'm taking you to a party."

The party was inside and outside a small two-storey building, about three minutes' walk in the warm evening air from Yael and Benjy's house.

"These are bed-sitting rooms for singles," Kobi explained.

A loudspeaker blared. A few people danced; others sat on crates and drank beer. Kobi grinned at her, left for a moment and came back with cold beers for both of them. He held her hand and dragged her round to meet some of his friends. It was too noisy to talk. He put his arm round her waist. They danced for a while, and then he steered her so they were standing under a tree. He held her tightly, and she wanted to run her fingers through his black curls.

"So, Dina. Tell me the truth because I see it in your eyes anyway. You came here because you are looking for an Israeli to marry."

"In England, no one would say that when they'd just met." She was giggling.

"I have this question about what happens in England. Tell me, Dina, how do they manage to keep their lips stiff when they kiss?"

She laughed. "You're ridiculous."

He pulled a face, an expression that was a caricature of a rabbit-toothed snob. "No, don't laugh. Show me." He leant towards her, holding her chin.

As their lips touched, an ear-piercing wail suddenly surrounded them.

"Shit, the siren. Quick. Run with me."

Kobi dragged her along a path.

"What's happening?"

"Hezbollah is sending Shabbat greetings," he said.

Denise could not understand where they were going. She saw parents carrying small children, older children in their pyjamas, and an old man with a walking stick hobbling as fast as he could. The people streamed through a door that was between some shrubs with *SHELTER* painted on it in Hebrew and English. Once inside, they went down steep stairs to an underground room. At first the air was refreshingly cool, but Denise quickly noticed a musty smell. People were still coming down the steps. Around her, little children were rubbing their sleep-filled eyes, or curled up on a parent's lap. People were whispering to each other so that they did not wake the babies. A little girl was dressing and undressing her doll. Two boys, who were about ten or eleven, were playing marbles in a small space that was free. No one but her seemed concerned.

Suddenly she was very scared. She hurled herself at Kobi and clung on to him. He stroked her shoulders.

"What's happening?" Denise asked. Her teeth were chattering.

"They've sent over a rocket or two. It's been quiet up here in the north for a while and the terrorists over the border are getting bored."

"How long do we have to stay down here?"

"Until we're told it's safe. We're all used to it. We

don't like it either, but that's the way it is. We're very near the Lebanese border."

"I've never been in a shelter before."

I don't know how they can live like this, she thought. She was crying and shaking. *How can they be so relaxed? We're all going to die.* Her chest was tight and she felt she would suffocate.

"I can't see you properly. Are you all right?" Kobi said.

"No. I can't breathe."

"This might help," he said, and he gently held her in his arms. "Breathe slowly and deeply. Listen to me, Dina. You're not going to suffocate. You're scared, but there's plenty of air and you're safe."

She did not believe him, but as she listened to him she felt calmer. The all clear sounded and they clambered back up into the night.

He escorted her back to Benjy and Yael's house and squeezed her hand. "*Layla Tov*," he said. "Hebrew for 'goodnight'." Then he grabbed her, held her so tight she could not breathe and gave her a long, passionate kiss.

The sofa was narrow and hard. The echo of the siren, her lingering fears and the memory of being in Kobi's arms staved off sleep.

As the room lightened with the dawn, she read the titles of books on the shelves and looked at the porcelain figures in the small cabinet. Her grandmother's presence hovered on the edge of her memory.

TWENTY-SIX

Kobi revved up the motorbike as she clambered onto the pillion. "We're going to the beach," he said, handing her the helmet. "You said you want to run."

He drove too fast but in spite of her fear she was excited. She clung to his waist and settled her head against the muscles along his spine. The sea was calm and the sandy beach almost deserted. A few campers were waking up, and there were fishermen casting lines. They ran along the ribbon of wet sand at the water's edge, and small waves uncurled over their bare feet.

"You want to run to the white cliff, Dina? Not too far?" *Never too far for me*, she wanted to say, but she speeded up instead and so did he. His legs and arms were muscular. She glanced at him and noticed his easy, deep breathing. *He's fit and strong*, she thought, *and very good to look at*.

They stopped at a beach café near the parked motorbike. Kobi bent down to brush sand from his toes and Denise noticed the ginger hairs on his legs.

"Hi, gorgeous," he said as he straightened up.

While they drank coffee, he wriggled his toes on her bare feet. She pulled her foot away. He moved his hand towards hers across the slats of the table.

"What are you doing later on today?" he asked.

"I haven't got anything special planned," she answered, then yawned.

"You look tired. I will take you back to the kibbutz, to my aunt's house. Their plane was in the night and now you have your own place. Have a rest, and this afternoon, if you want, you can join me and my friends on the beach. We play a sort of beach game with no rules. It's fun."

She collapsed onto a double bed in a darkened room and slept until Kobi woke her by shaking her gently. For a few seconds she couldn't work out where she was or who he was.

She pulled a bikini from her rucksack and smothered herself in sun cream. On the motorbike she breathed in his sweaty smell. A thought ran through her mind as they sped to the beach. *I want this for the rest of my life: my own place, the sunshine and this gorgeous man.*

A group of Kobi's friends had rigged up a net, and they volleyed a ball to each other, ran, fell on the sand and drank beer until long after sunset.

Back at Yael's sister's house Denise began to poke around in drawers and cupboards. There was a huge landscape painting that dominated the living room. It looked rough and unfinished, not like Oma's art. There were green and brown patches in the foreground and a hint of water, maybe a lake, in the background. Its size and dark colours made it threatening. In the bedroom, a life-size nude, a woman with sagging breasts and a tired expression, hung over the bed. Denise did not like that either, especially the slabs of grey and purple that were used for the contours of her body.

She had just found the coffee when she heard footsteps and the door was flung open by Kobi. He hadn't said he was coming over.

"Hi. You want a drink first?" he asked, opening his aunt and uncle's drinks cabinet. "Beer or something stronger?"

She watched him.

"We have a drink and then we go to bed."

"But," she muttered, "it's their bedroom and I don't feel comfortable."

He smiled at her, with that irresistible twinkle. "You left Denise, the English girl, at the airport, Dina. This is what you want, isn't it?"

He poured a beer for both of them and led her to the bedroom.

It was night when she woke needing the bathroom. As she got back to bed, he opened his eyes.

"Let's eat something," he said, and bounded out of the bed totally naked. He scrounged in the fridge and fed her with slices of cheese and grapes while she lay with the sheet pulled up.

"More of the good stuff." He pulled her on top of him as they tumbled.

Was she dreaming when she heard a strange, distant sound which could have been an animal howling or a call to dawn prayers? It was still dark outside. She and Kobi had dozed off with arms and legs entwined. She kissed his forehead and gently ran her fingers through his hair.

The bright sunlight finally woke her and she reached out her hand, but he was not there. She called him. Maybe he was in the bathroom, but there was no answer.

TWENTY-SEVEN

Benjy invited Denise to have breakfast with him in the kibbutz dining room. The communal dining room at Rylands School was a place where one ate quickly at allocated times. However, on the kibbutz, the dining room was the location for long and heated discussions during and after meals. From the first moment they had met she had not been sure what to make of Benjy. On the rare occasions that he smiled at her, it was no more than a fleeting movement of his lips. He was English and Peter's friend, and her expectation had been that she would be able to ask him questions. But Benjy bombarded her with questions instead. When they had walked past each other on one of the paths and he had not even acknowledged her, she had muttered out loud, "Don't you have any manners at all?"

That morning he sat on his own, dipping torn pieces of bread into two fried eggs. She put down her breakfast tray opposite him. He continued to concentrate intently on his eggs. She was tense, and thought she would choke if she ate even a mouthful of the cold scrambled egg on her plate.

He finally wiped his plate clean with another slice of bread, pushed it away and without looking at her said, "You've been here nearly a week."

"Five days, actually."

"And you're going back to England at the end of next week?" He started to dig into a bowl of chopped tomatoes and cucumbers. "When are you leaving the kibbutz?"

He's unbelievably rude, she thought.

"I'm not sure. I like it here and I'm thinking of staying a bit longer," she said.

"And where were you planning to live?" he asked, drumming his fingers on the table.

"Couldn't I stay in Yael's sister's house till they come back? I'm watering the plants for them."

"This isn't a hotel, Denise."

Her face was hot and her eyes prickled. "Thank you for the explanation, Benjy."

His expression did not change.

"I'm going to visit my relatives in Haifa tomorrow. And I've just decided that I'll find a place to stay there for a couple of days," she said. "When I come back to the kibbutz, I'll make arrangements to work as a volunteer."

Benjy threw back his head and laughed. His eyes watered and his body shook. She was humiliated and furious. "Sorry, girlie," he said, still spluttering. "It doesn't work like that here."

"If there's a problem with being a volunteer, I'll look for a job."

He laughed even louder. "You'll do what?"

How dare he talk to her like this? She stood, picked up her breakfast tray, her food untouched, and started to walk away.

He pulled her back. "Sit down, Dina, and let me explain. You don't understand. You're a visitor. You don't even speak the language. I've got no idea what kind of work you had in mind but they're not lining up to employ you."

"I've got a degree in sport and I'm trained to work with young people." She was thinking this out as she spoke. "It's the summer holidays. There must be camps for the children. I'm trained to coach swimming and tennis. Does that answer your question?"

And, she said silently to herself, *the answer to the question you haven't asked is that I'm not going to leave Kobi.*

Benjy got up to leave the table, put his hand on her shoulder and said, "We'll do what we can to help. Here it depends on who you know, not what you know. *Protektzia*, that's what it's called."

He stood for a few seconds. "You're a strange girl. You're like your mother. She came here on her own to find out something that was important to her. You'd make a go of it if you decided to stay." He put his breakfast dishes near the communal dishwasher.

Why go back to England, to chilly autumn and wet winter? She could start building her career right here. She strolled back to the house she was staying in, daydreaming of a future where she spoke Hebrew and lived with Kobi.

She was doing push-ups when Yael knocked on the door of the house and invited Denise to help her with work in the greenhouse during the morning.

They talked as they pruned and weeded. "Benjy talked to you, yes? The principal at the local high school is a friend of mine. I asked her if she could find work for you. Maybe help the students with English? They will finish the summer holiday in two weeks. She says it may be possible because one of the teachers is going to have a baby. Here on the kibbutz, there is bureaucracy with the volunteers. Better that you volunteer at the school. Let me know quickly."

"I would prefer to do something with sport."

Yael gave her a sharp look. "You are lucky we are helping you."

"I didn't know what it would be like here, Yael. I didn't expect to want to stay longer."

"You like it here? This is a little community where we grow things and we have a small factory. I don't understand what you like about it. If I went to England, I would see all the places like Buckingham Palace, the Houses of Parliament and the British Museum."

"I'm not sure why I like it here."

"I remember your mother, Dina." Yael handed her secateurs. "That's right. Prune it from where it joins the main stem."

"What did she do when she was here?" Denise asked, concentrating on what she was doing.

"Peter and Margot's baby cried a lot at night. She took him for walks round the kibbutz in the day so Margot could catch up on her sleep."

"Did she enjoy being here?"

"She wasn't here for long. In the evenings, your mother, Gabby, and I went for walks round the kibbutz. She talked a lot about her little baby girl; your first smile, how you loved splashing in the bath. Things that mothers talk about with other mothers."

"Do you think she was sorry she left me behind? She could have taken me with her."

"She knew your grandmother would take very good care of you and…" Yael stopped.

"And what, Yael? Go on, and what?"

"I'm trying to remember. She said something about promising your father. She promised him she would go back to England."

"Did she tell you that she wanted to live here?"

"She said your father would never agree to come here to live."

"He hasn't changed his mind. He tried his best to stop me coming."

"After what happened to your mother, who can blame him?"

They worked together until lunchtime.

TWENTY-EIGHT

"Vera's granddaughter. I can't believe it." Frieda reached up and pecked Denise lightly on each cheek. *I wouldn't want to hug her*, Denise thought. She followed the thin, upright figure of Frieda as she marched on high heels into the salon.

"Your journey? How was it? You found my address easily? You will have coffee?"

Frieda, like Benjy, interrogated. She pointed to where Denise should sit and announced that first she would bring coffee and cake, and only after that would they talk and she would bring out photo albums.

"There is so much I want to show you."

Her short legs were shapely and her hair looked like she had just come from the hairdresser. Frieda went to the kitchen and Denise looked round the room. It reminded her of Elizabeth's sitting room in London. Like Elizabeth, Frieda belonged to another place and time. Persian rugs in reds and salmon colours covered shiny wooden floorboards and there was a mahogany baroque dining table and chairs.

Frieda emerged wheeling a small trolley. "You take sugar? Brown or white? You will have cream with the strudel?" She sipped her coffee and stared at Denise, who fidgeted and noticed that there was a small stain on her T-shirt. She pushed back a stray curl. Frieda offered her more strudel. "One slice is nothing, Denise. The strudel is very good. I buy it from the best pastry shop in Haifa. Hungarians, of course."

Denise took a second slice.

"From where did you get the red hair?" Frieda questioned.

"No one knows," she replied.

"Leah, my daughter, has red hair, but hers comes from a bottle."

Denise laughed, but Frieda's thin lips remain pinched together.

"Old people do not receive many visitors." She reported this as if it was a fact of life. "I am happy you came to see me, Denise. You are a beautiful young woman. Dennis? What is that? It is a boy's name."

"Please call me Dina."

"I will try. You will remind me if I forget."

"What would you like me to call you? Cousin Frieda? Aunt Frieda?"

"I think Cousin Frieda would be right. And now, before I bring the photo albums, you will tell me what you are doing here in Israel."

"I wanted to see the country, but more than that I wanted to meet my relatives."

Frieda nodded her head slowly. "I think you have a special link with this country."

Denise did not know what to say. She wriggled on the chair.

"Of course I know what happened. Your mother visited me when she was here. She sat on that chair where you are sitting now. You do not look like her. You have a lot of relatives in England on your father's side of the family?" Frieda asked.

"My father has a brother who lives in Israel. I hope to meet him."

"Vera loved you very much." Frieda chose what to talk about, and Denise felt uncomfortable. "I have letters she wrote about you. She told me all the details. I know when you learned to walk, what were your first words. How sometimes you did not want to eat things Vera had cooked. You would like to see the letters?"

"Are they in German?"

"Yes, of course. But it would be easy to get them translated. Vera would have liked you to have them."

"Thank you."

"It was such a story, how Vera and I found each other after the war. I would like to tell you. But on another visit. Not today; I think you want to see photos of your grandmother as a little girl, yes?"

She did not wait for an answer but brought two dark leather photo albums and put them on the dining table. "It is better that we sit here so I can show you."

Denise turned the pages: two smiling, pudgy-cheeked little girls aged maybe nine or ten are holding hands and standing in the snow outside a mountain lodge. A family group sits at a table; the children are closest to the photographer, while parents and grandparents lean in to be included in the picture. Denise recognised Oma's grandfather, the rabbi. A round-faced little girl stands stiff and self-conscious next to her mother. The father has a fine-waxed moustache and a stern expression.

"Here is your grandmother with her parents and her baby brother." Frieda spoke quietly and slowly. "She must have been about five or six. And this cheeky little fellow is her baby brother, Fritz." Her face clouded over. "The photo is in black and white. Fritz had red hair."

Denise felt that she had been hit in the chest.

Frieda snapped the photo albums shut and stared at the carpet. "From all this family, only three of us survived. Your grandmother, my younger brother and me. All the others – the children, their parents, the old people – they were eaten up by Hitler. Austria has beautiful scenery but terrible people. They are such anti-Semites."

Denise did not break the silence that lasted for two or three minutes.

"My parents sent my brother and me to Palestine in 1936."

"Does your brother live in Haifa?" Denise asked.

"No. He went to America when he was a young man. He lived in New York. He passed away about the same time as Vera. That was a bad year."

Denise saw the lines on Frieda's face and dared to ask her about Palestine when she was a child. "This country must be so different from how it was when you came."

Frieda took her time. "Dina, you have no idea. You look around now and you see a modern country. We had ration books then. But we managed. And now there are cars and terrible traffic jams and I don't know what. This wasn't even a country when we came. And now we have everything. And still people are not satisfied."

Frieda sat upright on her chair. She stopped talking. She had heard something that excited her, and her face brightened. The next moment, Denise heard a voice calling from the front door. "My granddaughter Evie. She's forgotten her door key again. I want you to meet her." She walked to the door with outstretched arms.

A willowy, beautiful girl lit up the room with her voice and her dark eyes.

Frieda presented her. "Evie, my darling. Meet your cousin Dennis – I mean, Dina."

The shining eyes surveyed Denise and Evie stretched out her arms. "Hi, cousin." Denise was swept up into a bear hug.

"You speak English," Denise says.

"Sure. I'm half American. Savta, I bought you mangoes. They're perfect. Isn't Savta amazing? You're from England?"

"Evie, you remember I told you about my cousin Vera who was her grandmother? We grew up together in Vienna."

"And she came all this way to see you?" Turning to Denise, she asked, "Has my *savta* been telling you tales of long ago?" She rushed into the kitchen without waiting for an answer and came back biting into an apple. "She's got thousands of photos. I've never worked out how she managed to get them here from Vienna." Evie's hair and clothes floated and flowed. Beads swayed, earrings dangled. "So, Dina, what really brings you here? Curiosity about your relatives and the country, I suppose."

Frieda clasped one hand of each girl and stood between them. She was half a head shorter than both of them. She squeezed their hands. "My Evie is so full of love."

"Where are you staying?" Evie asked Denise. "Have you been to Haifa before?"

"No. This is my first time in Israel."

"Wonderful." Everything delighted Evie. "Why don't you stay with me for a few days at my mom's place? She hardly ever uses the apartment and never uses the spare room. We're next-door neighbours to Savta."

Frieda began to hustle the girls out of her apartment. "You've had enough of an old lady for one day. Go, children, enjoy yourselves."

Denise was enchanted. It was a similar feeling to being with her Manchester family. *My people*, she thought as she listed them: cousin Frieda, the photographs of Oma as a child, the little boy with red hair and this new cousin-sister, Evie.

Evie opened the door of the neighbouring apartment, which had a different outlook since it was on the opposite side of the building. The bright, spacious living room had a huge picture window overlooking Haifa Bay. A jumble of furniture filled the room and Denise did not know if she was in a home or a furniture showroom. The ceiling was high and the room was cool.

"Dump your backpack in the guest room," Evie ordered.

The guest room was mostly white with a pale cream rug. There was a white en-suite bathroom with a large printed-tile peacock on the wall.

"I'm in the kitchen," Evie called. "What do you want to eat?"

Denise stepped into a white-tiled kitchen that looked like a hospital clinic.

"My mother's not here. I live in Jaffa but I'm here for a few days most weeks. There's cheese, olives, bread and some leftover pasta."

They sat perched on high stools at the small white table.

"If our grandmothers were first cousins, what does that make us? I'm not much good at family tree stuff," Evie said. She spoke with an American accent and nibbled the olives.

"Neither am I," Denise answered.

"Hey, Dina, why did you come here? Really?"

"I want to see the country and meet relatives."

"You came with a group?"

"No. I came on my own."

"Then I don't believe you. There is something special that you want to discover. People who want to see the country come with a group, stay at hotels and go round in a bus with a tour guide. Or if they're young, they come with a youth group and go to camp. So what's the secret, Dina? Are you exploring the idea of settling here?"

"Evie, I can't answer your questions. There's so much I don't know about this place."

"You said this is the first time you've been here?"

Denise nodded.

"How long have you been here?"

"A week."

"That's nothing. And what do you think so far?"

"It's noisy. People are rude. I don't speak Hebrew. And I love it here."

"How long are you staying?"

"I told my father I would only stay for two weeks."

Evie put her head on one side. "That's ridiculous. How can you begin to know anything in two weeks? All by yourself, in this crazy land where you don't speak the language." She laughed and put her arm around Denise. "Tell me more. I'm so curious."

"I have a problem."

Evie nodded. "Go on."

"I promised my dad that I'd only be here for two weeks and I'm due to go home next week. I don't want to go back so soon."

"You only have to change your ticket. It might be expensive, though."

"You don't understand. It's because of my dad."

"He's sick?"

"No. He didn't want me to come because he says it's not safe here. My mum was…"

"I know what happened."

"My dad made me promise to come for only two weeks and now…"

"But, Dina, you're not a child. You're old enough to make your own decisions. How old are you? I'm twenty-two."

"Twenty-one. My dad is one of the world's best worriers and most of his worries are focused on me."

"Oh my God. I get it. He's terrified he might lose you like he lost your mother. Or that you'll fall in love with an Israeli and stay here. Did your dad marry again?"

"I don't get on with my stepmother."

"You can't go back before you've sorted things out a bit. And you definitely can't go back because your dad says so."

"You don't know what he's like."

"Of course I do. He's a Jewish mother, except he's your father. I'm going to tell you what you must do." Evie placed the phone in Denise's hand. "Phone him now. Tell him you've just met your cousin and she's going to keep you safe and take you around the country."

"I can't do that."

"You can, but you've decided that you won't."

"No. You only met me half an hour ago. You don't know him at all."

Evie gazed at her across the table and put her chin in her hands. "I don't want to upset you, Dina. I'm so excited to discover a cousin. The only other cousin I have is on my father's side and he lives in LA."

Denise took a deep breath. "He's always... I mean, he thinks about..."

"Poor man. He must have loved your mother very much."

"He never talks about her."

Evie took her hand across the table. "Because it hurts him too much. And you remind him of her. Do you look like her?"

"My *oma* said that I don't look like her at all, but that the way I talk and think is like her."

Evie nodded. "You don't want to hurt him, do you?"

"Exactly."

Evie squeezed her hand. "When you've argued with him in the past, does he get over it?"

"I can often talk him round, but it was different with coming here. He wouldn't budge unless I promised that it was only for two weeks."

"And for you, Dina – what's the worst thing that will happen if you decide to go home now?"

The worst thing, she thinks quickly, would be not to see Kobi again. "I'll speak to him," she said.

Denise tapped the phone. It rang a few times before her father picked up.

"Hi, Dad."

"Denny." Her father was excited, and spoke so loudly that she had to hold the phone away from her ear. "I'll be there at the airport on Thursday. I've got a special surprise for you."

"Dad, I have to tell you something," she blurted.

"I'm listening."

"It's not what I expected here and I… er… I…"

"You want to come home tomorrow? Not a problem."

"No, Dad. I want to stay a bit longer."

"You want to stay a bit longer?"

"I'd rather you came home." His voice was commanding.

"I don't want to come home yet, Dad. I know what I want."

"What's made you change your mind?"

Evie signalled to her. "Keep saying the same thing," she whispered.

"Dad, I've made up my mind and I want to stay a bit longer."

Evie gave a thumbs-up.

"What's made you change your mind?" he repeated.

"I told you, Dad. It's different from what I expected. I don't know anything about this country and I want to stay longer."

Evie went into the kitchen and came back with scissors.

"You're in a country where you might get blown up any minute by terrorists. That's enough for me to know that you should come home."

"I'm in Haifa, Dad, and I'm having a good time with my cousin, Evie."

"Who's this Evie? I want to talk to her."

She held her hand over the mouthpiece. "He wants to talk to you," she said. Evie shook her head. "Her grandmother was Oma's first cousin. She's about my age. I'm here in her mother's apartment. There's a view across—"

He cut her short.

"I don't like it, Denny," he said. "Not at all. I worry about you all the time."

She took a deep breath. "You don't have to worry, Dad. I'll keep in touch."

"You'll phone me every evening, you hear? Every evening."

"It will be more like twice a week, Dad."

"And you won't go on buses? Or sit in cafés?"

"Dad…" she says.

"Yes, Denny, stay in touch."

She closed the phone. "Any more of that wine, Evie? What's with the scissors?"

"I thought you might need to cut the umbilical cord."

They laughed.

Five minutes later, Denise's mobile phone rang.

"Dad? Why are you phoning back?" she asked.

"You haven't told me what you're doing. I don't even know the people you're staying with." He sounded angry and bitter.

"I'm twenty-one. You managed without me when I was at boarding school and university. I'm not a little girl any more."

"You're still *my* little girl. I missed you all those years. Who are all these exciting relatives you've suddenly discovered?"

"I told you. Oma came from a big family."

He doesn't say anything.

"Before she got out of Austria she used to spend her holidays with her cousin Frieda, and I went to see her. She's—"

"You spend your time with your *oma*'s family, and when are you going to meet my brother?"

"This is my mother's family. You said you didn't want me to meet your brother."

"There's a lot I could say about the subject, but I won't."

"You told me about your brother Barry, and how he cheated you and your parents. I'm not sure that I want to meet him anyway."

"I didn't say that he cheated us. He saw an opportunity to do what mattered to him and he took it."

"That wasn't how you told me, Dad."

"Listen, Denny," he said. "When all is said and done, family is family, isn't it?"

"Are you saying that you want me to contact him?"

"I don't want to burden you, and maybe you don't want to but—"

"Get to the point, Dad."

"You've got the phone number. Call him on Friday. Wish him a good Shabbos. Tell him I send my best wishes. That's all I want you to do. If he wants to invite you, that's up to him."

"I'll think about it, Dad."

"Of course, of course. I'm not pushing you, Denny."

"I'll let you know what he says; that is, if I do decide to call him."

"It's the least I can do for my parents, may they rest in peace."

TWENTY-NINE

The next morning, Denise and Evie were sprawled in the cluttered living room, watching from the windows of the apartment building, high on the ridge of the Carmel, as tiny cars drove along the coast and toy commercial boats were anchored in Haifa Bay.

"Now you've talked to your father, what are you going to do, Dina?" Evie pushed her long, sleek hair from her face.

"Get a job for a few months and see how things work out."

"What things? A guy? Already?"

Denise took a deep breath and wondered where to begin. "He's a mechanic. He fixes motor bikes and he lives on the kibbutz."

"And he's the most amazing, handsome guy you've ever met?"

"He makes me laugh and he's different from any of the blokes I went out with in England."

"And you changed your plans because of him?"

"Yes and no. When we're together it's like I feel he's

exactly what I was looking for without even knowing that I was looking."

Evie coiled her hair and fixed it with a large clip on top of her head. She rearranged her slim body so that her feet were curled under her. "He's worked on you, Dina. He's used, or should I say oozed, charm and now you're the cobra and all he has to do is play on his flute and you'll do whatever he wants. More coffee?"

"No thanks, Evie. I just… I didn't come here to…"

"How did you meet him?"

Denise told her about the bus ride and the coincidence that he was Benjy's son.

"He took advantage of you, Dina. You'd just arrived. These coincidences happen all the time. This is a small country and he made the most of it; made you feel that something special was happening."

"You're right, but I think about him all the time."

"Does he think about you all the time? What's your guess?"

"He works hard. He's busy."

"These Israeli men. They're so sure of themselves. They think the only reason girls come to this country is to have sex with them."

Denise blushed.

"Let me guess. He got you into bed the first day you were here." Evie clicked her tongue and sighed as if she'd heard all this before. "And now you're waiting by a silent phone?"

Denise said, "It's not only him."

"Go on."

186

"It's being here. It's not what I expected. I mean, the country, the kibbutz, meeting family. I keep asking myself how I can feel so at home when I didn't grow up here and I don't speak Hebrew. And I've only been here eight days. But I've never felt like this, ever."

"A sense of connection?"

"That's exactly right. And then Benjy said to me that I'm the sort of person who would make a go of it if I decided to stay. And now suddenly I've decided to stay. It's like something bigger and stronger than me is making decisions."

"And what?" Evie asked.

"This sounds weird. I keep asking myself if my mother is somehow making this happen. Isn't that spooky?"

"So it's a love affair with a fantastic man and finding your destiny all in five days?"

"Is that ridiculous?"

Evie looked serious. "Let's take this slowly." Denise relaxed a little. "First, it isn't ridiculous. There are different levels to our lives and a lot of the time we're not even aware of what's going on inside us. Second, it's not surprising you feel a sense of connection. You're Jewish. You know enough about Jewish history to understand that Jews need a homeland like other nations. Your mother, from what you've told me, felt that so strongly that she left you and came here. Third, you've been here less than a week. Recognise that you are in love with a man and with the country. Enjoy the honeymoon phase. The intense passion blinds us but it never lasts. It's like a bright flame and it has to die down and melt into something else. If you're right for each other, it will be clearer as time passes. If not, you'll have memories that will always make you smile."

"You should be a teacher."

"I tried. It wasn't my thing."

"There's one more thing," Denise said. "I want to buy a pair of sandals like yours."

"We'll go to the market."

They were tired and sticky when they got back to the apartment.

Evie fumbled for the front door key and sniffed. "My mother's here. She smokes."

The TV was switched on. A woman with long red hair whose face Denise could not see sat with her feet on a footstool, cigarette between her fingers. Without turning her head, she shouted at Evie in Hebrew, long strings of guttural noises interrupted by pauses when she lifted the cigarette to her lips. Evie brought her a glass of cold white wine. The woman continued to shout. Evie took the cigarette from her mother's fingers, sat next to her and began to stroke her hand and arm. Then she moved to stand behind her and massaged her neck and shoulders.

She spoke in English. "Deep breaths, Ima. You'll feel better soon."

Denise watched from near the door.

"Who's the lost soul you've brought in this time?" the woman said in English. "This place isn't a hotel." Her voice was gravelly, her fingernails long and red.

Evie kept on with the massage. Denise thought she should leave, but Evie mouthed something that looked like 'wait'.

"Ima, this is Dina. She's my cousin and she's visiting from England. I invited her to stay and I'll take care of her. You don't have to do a thing."

"I'll go back to the kibbutz, I don't want to trouble you."

The woman turned towards her and pushed her long hair back from her worn, pale face. Her lips matched her red nails.

"What did you say your name was? Dina? I'm exhausted and I have a headache. Don't get the wrong impression. You can stay here. Evie will look after you. I'm going out in an hour. Who are your parents?" She talked without waiting for an answer. "Evie's always finding lost souls. She's a bleeding heart. You want to know why I'm so tired? I run a quality furniture store. The family business. But these days, it's all throwaway stuff. Quality? No one cares. They only want furniture that comes in boxes, so they can take it home in the car. The world's changed. I stand in the shop all day and how many customers do I get? How many?" she shouted. "Today, two people came into the shop and what did they buy? Nothing. Not a thing.

"Evie, bring me a Tylenol. You, whatever your name is, you bought those sandals at the market? What did you pay for them? I hope you bargained. You have to bargain with them. Arabs."

Evie came back with the pills and a glass of water. "Don't go out again, Ima. Have a shower and go to bed. You can watch TV and I'll bring you something to eat."

"I can't eat a thing."

Evie draped her mother's arm round her shoulder and led her to another room. When she came back sometime later, she flopped into an armchair.

"She's got problems. She can't cope with stress, and for her getting up in the morning is a crisis."

Denise was confused. "You live here with your mother? I thought you lived in Jaffa."

"It's complicated. This is her apartment but she goes to stay with her boyfriend most of the time. They must have had a row, which would explain why she was here and why she was in such a bad mood. You're right. I do live in Jaffa. I come here once a week if I can, to keep an eye on my mother."

"Where's your father?" Denise asked.

"Probably in Brazil. Do you mind if we stay in this evening, Dina, so I'm here for my mom if she gets upset again? I'll call her boyfriend in the morning and ask him why she's in such a state."

Denise wondered what she would do if her father were like Evie's mother. *I wouldn't have the patience.*

"Hey, Dina, tomorrow I'm going back to Jaffa. Why don't you come with and stay with me for a few days. You'll meet my friends. You'll love it there. You don't mind a mattress on the floor, do you?"

Evie's apartment in Jaffa was a huge room with a vaulted ceiling. Curtains, Indian fabrics and beads divided the space and hung from a criss-cross of string lines. Papers were piled next to an earthenware pot on an old kitchen table. A girl propped up on her elbows lay on a mattress.

She was scribbling and striking out passages in what appeared to be a script. She waved at them as they came in but was too busy to chat. There was a smell of fried onions and spices. Denise was enchanted.

Evie said, "That's Anat. The two of us share the apartment."

Later that evening, they went to a nearby basement to hear Eastern music. "Come on, Dina. Bring your drink downstairs."

Denise, one hand on the damp wall, the other clutching a long, cold drink laced with vodka, followed Evie down a narrow, dark staircase into a basement room lined with brick walls on which hung Indian fabrics like those in Evie's flat. A musty smell was partly masked by incense. People sat on large cushions on the floor.

Three men sat cross-legged on rugs on a small raised platform. One played soft beats on a drum. Another played a stringed instrument with more strings than a guitar and a different sound. The third blew on a kind of flute. The audience listened intently, but Denise found the music unfamiliar and repetitive. The drumbeats were irregular, the flute whined and there was no recognisable melody.

Evie whispered, "It grows on you."

The three men were dark, or maybe it was the poor lighting. One had a black moustache. They wore baggy, striped pants and sashes over their shoulders. The vodka began to have an effect and she let the music waft over her.

They walked back the short distance to the flat along a street lined with young children on scooters or playing with balls.

"It's so late. Don't the children go to bed here?" Denise asked.

"It's cooler in the evenings. Arab families enjoy the breeze."

The young man who ran to join them kissed and hugged Evie.

"Dina, meet Selim, my boyfriend. He played the oud."

"That was the instrument like a guitar?" Denise asked as she realised that Selim was one of the musicians.

"Did you like the music?" Selim asked her.

"Not at first," she answered.

Selim put his arm round Evie's waist and walked back to the flat with them.

That night, Denise lay awake. First she was too hot and then when she threw aside the sheet, she was too cold. She could still hear the strange music in her head. Evie was not like anyone she'd ever met before. She was bursting with life, as if every second had to be experienced or she might miss something. Denise wanted to ask her about Selim, about having an Arab boyfriend, but didn't know what to say. *Do many Jewish girls have Arab boyfriends? Can it be dangerous? How did she meet Selim? Is it OK to ask these questions?*

The next morning, when Evie was cutting bread, Denise blurted, "Does your mother know that your boyfriend is an Arab?"

"Darling Dina, you're too new here to begin to understand. First of all, my mother can't cope with anyone other than herself and she doesn't manage that very well. More important, and here comes another lecture, there's too much hate in this country. I grew up surrounded by hate. My mother hates my grandmother and my father. My grandmother hates my father. My father hates this country. Everyone hates the Arabs. I can't live like that."

Evie was holding Denise's hands and staring into her eyes. "I'm serious, darling, absolutely serious. It got so bad I cut my wrists when I was seventeen. Look at the scars. We have to mend ourselves and this country with love." She laughed. "You're looking at me as if I'm from another planet. Look at your stepmother. She's a bitch. You hate her. What does that do to you? To her? To your dad? Let your hate melt. She doesn't have to be your favourite person. The hate poisons you and doesn't make her any different. Love, love, love. It has to be the answer. Jews hate Arabs. Arabs hate Jews. They kill each other and still go on hating. Nothing changes. Selim loves Evie and Evie loves Selim. Two happy people. Understand?"

"No," said Denise. "But I'll think about it."

Evie was busy the next morning. Denise wanted to go to the beach.

"It's ten minutes walk or five minutes run to the beach in Tel Aviv. Enjoy. See you later." Evie told her.

Perfect, thought Denise, *I'm on holiday.* the noise, the sand, the heat, and smells of sunscreen, falafel and chips. Young men whose wares bulged in their skimpy swimsuits swarmed like flies around any unattached young woman. She joined that peculiar batting Israeli beach game with six or seven of them and three American girls. She swam, she ran on the sand, she started and finished conversations about nothing, she turned down cigarettes and joints.

"It's Friday, Dina, and if you plan to go back to the kibbutz you have to know that the buses stop running in the afternoon." Evie said when she got back to Jaffa.

"Hell," she replied, "I'm having such a good time."

"Stay here for Shabbat. No problem." Nothing was a problem for Evie.

"But maybe Kobi will be there…"

Evie shrugged. "Why do women make men the centre of their lives?"

"I know. It's stupid and I'm setting myself up to get hurt."

Evie shook her head. "Go to your lover. Drown in your passion. When you want me, you know where to find me."

THIRTY

Kobi was there at the bus stop to meet her. He grabbed her and kissed her so hard that she found it hard to breathe. "You go to Tel Aviv with your cousin and forget all about me?"

"But you disappeared. What did you want me to do?"

"Red-haired angel of mine, I can't resist you. We'll go to the Golan."

He did not ask her what she wanted to do, she noticed.

"If I drive too fast, tell me," he said as he helped her with the crash helmet. They roared away from the kibbutz with Denise clinging to Kobi's waist.

Through the goggles the landscape was a blur as they sped towards the road to the Golan Heights. *If this is the end*, she thought during the journey, *it's in the right place with the right man.*

"Isn't there a speed limit?" she asked when he pulled up in a gravel car park. Her knees were still shaking. She gave him the crash helmet.

"Limits? What are they? You weren't scared, were you?" He grinned. "You're safe with me." He parked the bike. "I'll show you something which will help you understand this place."

They were alone in a deserted army bunker. He led her through narrow concrete passages until they reached a cliff edge overlooking neat fields far below. Tiny figures walked from their houses towards Lake Galilee. A tractor stood in a field. A dot jumped up and down and Denise could hear a faint bark.

"Now you can sit and enjoy the view." He delved into his pack and brought out a thermos.

"Where are we?"

"That's Kibbutz Ein Gev. This was a Syrian bunker, and Syrian soldiers used to sit here and pick off anyone they wanted to. Easy."

"How could people live like that?"

"We all lived like that."

"But it must have been worse for those people in the kibbutz down there."

"A bit worse, but Tel Aviv was only twenty miles from the border before the Six Day War."

"Wouldn't it be better for everyone in the Middle East if Israel had made peace with the Arabs after that war?"

"The Arabs will never make peace. They don't want us here. As far as they're concerned we have no right to be here. For them, it doesn't matter if it takes generations; they want their land back. And this is our land. That's the conflict in two sentences."

"But how can—?"

He put his fingers over her lips. "There is no other way, Dina. We've only got one state and that's Israel. If we don't defend it, we'll lose it." He was more serious than she had ever seen him. "Some people believe that the God of Israel was on our side in the Six Day War."

"Is that what you believe?"

"Me?" He grinned. "I'm a simple soldier when I'm not fixing motorbikes. When I come here and it's quiet, I think that if we listen very carefully, we'll hear the ghosts of the soldiers shouting and screaming."

"Or maybe it's the wind," she said.

"We hear the wind with our ears. We hear the soldiers as they die with the ears of our hearts." His chin trembled.

She moved towards him and he put his arm around her. He pulled her to the ground and buried his face between her breasts.

Back at the little house where she was staying, Denise and Kobi sat naked on the bed, feeding each other morsels of cheese and drinking wine.

"I told my dad that I'm staying in Israel for longer."

He kissed her. "That's good."

"He wants me to visit his brother. He's got a jewellery shop in Jerusalem."

"Every time we talk, you tell me about another relative. Does he live in Jerusalem?"

"No. He lives in Kiryat Arba."

"Kiryat Arba!" Kobi jumped up and stamped the floor. "They'll invite you for Shabbos."

"So what?" Denise asked.

"There's no way I'm going to let you spend next Shabbat in Kiryat Arba," Kobi said. "First, it's dangerous to get to. Second, it's dangerous being there." He held up his fingers as he made the list. "Third, who knows, you may decide to join those religious extremists. I don't want to lose you."

"You don't tell me what I do and what I don't do."

"The people who live there, you don't know what they're like. Believe me, Dina, they're religious fanatics. You know what a fanatic is?"

"Don't patronise me. You know what 'patronise' means?"

"It's better that you meet your uncle for a coffee in Jerusalem. Then you can leave when you want. You want I phone him tomorrow?"

"No, Kobi. This is my family. They may not even invite me, so I don't know why you're making it into such a big deal. It's one day, that's all."

"That's their way. They're busy during the week. Shabbos means Friday afternoon to Sunday morning and that is more than one day."

"I'll come back on a bus."

He laughed. "There aren't any. You don't know what you're getting into. It's the Wild West except the men don't wear cowboy hats. Everyone goes round with a gun and they have God on their side."

"If I don't like it there, I'll find a way to leave."

"You won't be able to. No cars. No buses. If you go out of their sight, they'll worry that Arabs have kidnapped you. It's not London, Dina. It's the frontier."

"All right, I'll stick it out. How bad can it be? I know the Shabbat rules. I grew up with them. I'll take a book. Benjy lent me *Exodus*. You know that book?"

He relaxed. "That book is corny. The country isn't like that any more. And Paul Newman isn't like that any more, either."

She looked at him, relaxed and tapping his fingers on the table. *You think you can make all the rules, don't you?* she thought.

"Why do you think I'm going to Kiryat Arba?" she said.

"I listen, Dina. You are doing what the children in this country do when they are preparing for their bar mitzvah. You're exploring your roots."

THIRTY-ONE

"Who wants him?" a girl's voice asked Denise when she phoned her Uncle Barry's home.

"I'm a visitor from England and we're related," she replied.

"He'll be home this evening after eight." The conversation ended.

A woman answered when she phoned that evening. "Who are you and how did you get this number?" She spoke sharply and had an American accent.

"Is this Barry Levisohn's home?" Denise asked.

"Who is this?" the woman hissed.

"My father is Graham Levisohn, Barry's brother," Denise said.

There was a pause. *She's put her hand over the phone and she's talking to someone.* "My husband doesn't have a brother. You've made a mistake."

"Don't hang up yet... please," Denise said.

"I've told you. My husband doesn't have a brother."

"Can I talk to him, please?"

"One moment." The hand went over the phone again and there were inaudible mutterings.

A man's voice, deep and strong with an accent like her father's. "Whoever you are, you've called a wrong number."

"I'm looking for someone who is, or used to be, called Barry Levisohn."

"What do you want him for?" At least he hadn't hung up.

"My father asked me to deliver his greetings for a peaceful Sabbath."

The man snorted. "And you've come all the way from England to do that? What a devoted daughter."

"Who am I speaking to?"

"Baruch Levi."

"Do you want me to call you Uncle Baruch or Uncle Barry?"

"Hang on."

The hand over the phone must be the way they make arrangements, she thought.

"My wife wants me to ask you if you can come to us for Shabbos?"

"Not this week," she said quickly to give herself time.

"Next week? I work in Jerusalem. Come to my shop on Friday morning and we'll go home together. What did you say your name was?"

"Dina."

She wrote down the address of his shop.

Is it only two weeks since I was here in Jerusalem? It feels like I've been in this country for months. Should I have brought a present? A bottle of wine? She looked around for the side street where her uncle's shop was located. Near Ticho House, Benjy had told her.

The big man hunched behind the counter was working with a jeweller's eyepiece. He continued to concentrate on what he was doing while Denise looked round. Pendants with precious stones, mostly diamonds, were displayed in locked glass cabinets on glass shelves with mirror backing. Prices were hard to find. She sat on one of the black padded seats. The jeweller took out his eyeglass, stood up and rubbed his protruding stomach. He was tall, stout and had a thick red beard.

"With that hair, you can only be my niece," he boomed. He stroked his beard. "You want a glass of water?" As he turned to get the water for her, she noticed the fringes he wore over his trousers and the side-curls tucked behind his ears. "My wife will be here in about half an hour and then we'll drive home. Why don't you get yourself a coffee and come back?"

She left her rucksack at the shop, bought an ice cream and wandered along a traffic-free street where groups of excited American teenagers jostled each other, each one talking loudly with no one listening. The shops were aimed at the tourist trade. T-shirts with slogans about Israel and arrays of skullcaps filled the windows.

Her uncle was closing the shop when she got back. An adolescent boy was helping him. A plump woman sat on the black leather chair and leaned on her shopping trolley.

"This is my son Arieh and my wife Hannah. Everyone ready? Let's get going."

Arieh reminded Denise of Felix. He had acne and stared resolutely out of the car window. The radio played religious music interrupted by news. Hannah and Barry talked non-stop in Hebrew.

They left Jerusalem. The car crawled along in the traffic. Denise watched as the scene abruptly changed from apartment buildings to open, rocky land. Soldiers waved them through a checkpoint. The road began to wind through low hills and olive groves. There were occasional small stone houses by the roadside with courtyards shaded by vines. The scene was pastoral. Denise wanted to ask who the houses belonged to but felt shut out by the heated conversation in the front seat and Arieh's back.

They drove into the wide streets of Kiryat Arba with its modern multi-storey buildings. Denise looked at the women, their heads covered with scarves as they rushed along with strollers and gaggles of small children. Men with skullcaps or large black hats and fringes over their trousers strolled through the streets. Most of them had bushy beards.

The car drew up in the car park of a tall apartment building. Hannah suddenly demanded, in a loud American voice, "Help me with the shopping, will you?" She handed Denise a heavy bag and the shopping trolley from the car boot.

Denise followed her into the first-floor flat. The front door was scratched and the paint in the hall passage was flaking. There were posters with religious themes stuck to the walls with tape. A skinny, pale girl, who had to be one of Denise's cousins, grabbed the shopping trolley from her and started packing the food into a double-door refrigerator. Another girl, plump like her mother, called out to Denise. "Hey, Dina. I'm Tehila. Come and help me set the table. We'll be twenty people tonight."

Normal people, thought Denise, *have ways of introducing themselves to someone they've never met before.*

"I'd like to dump my rucksack and wash my hands and face first."

"Oh, yeah, sorry. Third door on the right is the bathroom and we've put a mattress for you in our bedroom. The room next to the bathroom."

The bedroom was crowded and untidy with bedclothes all over the floor. The wardrobe doors were open. She went to help Tehila.

As the afternoon wore on, the apartment door was left open. Women, girls and younger children began to arrive and make themselves at home. No one took any notice of Denise. Hannah bustled around shouting orders until she gathered her daughters to light the Shabbat candles. When the men returned from evening prayers, everyone took their places at the table. Tehila told Denise to sit between her and the pale, skinny girl, who whispered that she was called Avigail. Denise had not eaten since breakfast. The smell of soup pervaded the room and her stomach rumbled. Blessings and songs went on endlessly. Tehila fussed over her when the meal was served, urging her to try the dishes, especially the ones she'd cooked. Her other cousins chatted to their girlfriends in Hebrew. Their mothers were American and spoke loudly. Denise caught snatches of their conversations.

"I usually do the brisket for at least four hours on a slow oven."

"It was measles. I was sure he'd already had it."

"Those mad checkpoint women were talking to the soldiers again this morning."

At the other end of the table the men were praying or arguing vigorously.

During the night, Denise listened to jackals howling and the muezzin calling. Later, her cousins began to stir. For a few seconds, she was tempted to put on her running shoes and get out of the flat. It was the morning of the day of rest, Shabbat, and she did not know the customs of the family. She lay on her mattress, watching the girls brushing their long hair. Tehila asked her if she wanted to come to the synagogue with them. "Or you can go later by yourself if you want."

Being stuck in a synagogue is the last thing I want to do, Denise thought.

"Thank you, but I prefer to stay here and read."

"Sure. No one locks the door on Shabbat. We're very safe here. There's a fence and the soldiers guard us."

The family left for their morning prayers and Denise went out for a walk. The streets were quiet with a background noise of chanting voices from the synagogues. Soldiers guarded the main entrance to the settlement. She nodded to them and wished them Shabbat Shalom.

"Am I allowed to speak to you?" she said to two soldiers who stood near her.

"What do you want to know?" The young soldier spoke with an American accent.

"I'm visiting some relatives who live here. I didn't realise that this place was so religious."

He laughed. "You need to ask your relatives about that. Kiryat Arba is mentioned at the beginning of the Bible."

"I've got a lot to learn, haven't I?" she said. "But why the fence and the guards? Is it so dangerous here?"

"If you're fighting for what you know is right, you sometimes have to make big sacrifices. Understand what I mean?"

"I think so. Tell me, who are the 'mad checkpoint women'? Someone talked about them last night."

"They're a bunch of leftie grandmothers who are out to cause trouble with the army and the government."

"Why?"

"Hey, are you having me on? You're either completely ignorant or completely dumb. They have this crazy idea that Israel should exchange land for peace."

"Isn't that a good idea?" She questioned.

"The Arabs will never want peace. They want the Jews out altogether."

She stared at this arrogant youth and then smiled. "You know something? I've learnt more from you in a couple of minutes than I have in two weeks in the country. Have a good Shabbat."

She strolled along an impressive promenade that ended at the grave of Dr Baruch Goldstein who, according to the inscription, was a holy martyr. Not keen to return to the apartment, she sat under a tree and read her book for a while. She must have dozed off, because she became aware of waves of voices. Services must be over and she should go back for lunch.

"Who was Baruch Goldstein?" she asked Avigail when the two of them were alone in the bedroom.

"He's one of our heroes. But not everyone thinks so."

"Tell me why he's a hero."

"I don't want to." Avigail looked even more miserable.

"Should I ask Tehila?" Denise said.

"No. Don't. She'll get upset. She thinks what he did was wrong. She'll tell you that he murdered Arabs."

Her uncle was drinking lemon tea, and looked up from the book he was reading. "Is there a way I can get back to Jerusalem tonight?" Denise asked.

"Hannah," he shouted, "is anyone driving to Jerusalem tonight? The niece wants to go back."

Hannah emerged from another room. She frowned at Denise. "There's more to see here than just your uncle and his family. The holiest place in Judaism is just down the road. Obviously, you don't know and you don't care."

Religious fanatics, Denise thought. *Kobi was right.*

"At my Jewish day school I was told that worshipping buildings is a form of idolatry."

"Well, well, the redhead apparently has had some kind of Jewish education, Baruch," Hannah said in a snide voice.

"That's enough, Hannah. She's a guest here and she's my niece. Do you know if anyone is driving to Jerusalem this evening?"

"Not as far as I know."

"I'm driving there tomorrow to work and to take Arieh back to the yeshiva. We will leave at seven."

Arieh sat in the front seat. When he got out of the car, he waved feebly in Denise's direction.

"Stay in the back of the car," Baruch said to her. "There's too much traffic to stop here for more than a few seconds. I'm parking near the shop. We'll be there in ten minutes if the traffic stays like this."

"That's good for me."

Baruch hooted at a taxi. A bus was pulling out and was very close to the car.

"Well?" he shouted at her. "Did you get what you came for?"

"I wanted to meet you."

"That's what your mother said when she came into my shop."

"My mother? She was only in the country for a week. Did she come to see you at the beginning of her visit or at the end?"

"I didn't invite her. She just turned up. I looked at her and thought about my brother, about our parents. How could he have married a woman like that?"

"My father's observant."

"She was dressed like a trollop. I wanted to throw her out. I asked her what she wanted. She said to me, 'Your brother Graham is a good man.' Those were her very words. Then she marched out of the shop, down the street, and about twenty minutes later there was a boom. At that time, we all knew what those booms were. Another suicide bomber."

"You were the last one to see her?" Denise whispered. "Why do you think she came to your shop?"

He did not answer. He took long, deep breaths.

Eventually he said, "She wanted to remind me that it was your father who had helped me to lead my life the way I wanted."

He pulled the car into a parking space in one of the narrow old streets near his shop.

"Thank you for your hospitality, Uncle Baruch. And for what you told me."

"May your mother's memory be blessed, Dina."

THIRTY-TWO

She asked directions for the café where she had arranged to meet Kobi. He wasn't there, and when she realised she was an hour early she ran round Independence Park. *My mother was here. She saw the places I am seeing, she talked to Yael and Benjy, met that fanatic uncle of mine and told him that he should be grateful to his brother. I can imagine her marching out of his shop, feeling pleased, thinking about what she would say to my dad. And then she went into that café, ordered a coffee and was blown into bits.* Denise sat on a park bench.

As she walked to meet Kobi, she thought again about her mother. *What did she plan to do when she got back to England? Was she going back to work? Was Oma going to look after me while she worked? Where was she working? She's more real to me now than she's ever been.*

Kobi was at the café.

"Not good, eh? You look awful." He kissed her. "You're shaking. It was that bad?"

"I'm glad I met them, Kobi, and I'm so happy to see you after the last two days."

"What was your uncle like?"

"A religious fanatic."

Kobi ran his fingers through his hair and stretched. "I was a soldier there for a bit."

"I'm hungry. Do they serve eggs with that spicy tomato sauce?"

Kobi ordered breakfast. "I get tense when I'm in Jerusalem. It's crammed with old buildings and old ideas. We're not spending the day here. I'm showing you more of the country."

A young American wearing jeans and carrying a gun joined them at the table.

"Dina, this is my friend, Haim." Kobi gave him a hug. "So, how're things?"

Haim had a crocheted blue-and-white skullcap on his light brown hair. He was suntanned, wiry and about the same age as Kobi.

"Haim's a tour guide. I've taken a few days off work and we're going on a *tiyul*."

"A what?" she asked.

"It's a hike," Haim said.

When Denise wiped the last spot of delicious spicy *shakshuka* from her plate, she asked where they were going.

"You'll see, and you'll love it," Haim said.

Haim drove his jeep out of Jerusalem on a main road into a desert of dusty hills. Small herds of goats scratched the sand for vegetation. A group of shacks made of sheets of corrugated iron nestled in a hollow. Washing flapped, but there were no people. As they drove on, a boy riding bareback galloped across the hills towards the shacks.

"Bedouin," Haim commented.

They swung off the road at a brown signpost.

"Ein Prat Nature Reserve or Wadi Qelt," Haim explained. "We'll park here and hike through the wadi. Tonight, we'll stay with friends of mine and they'll drive us back to the car in the morning."

"Why have you both got guns?" she asked.

"Don't worry. It's safe. But there were one or two unpleasant incidents a few years ago," Kobi explained.

A narrow river bubbled over rocks in the bed of a gorge. "The River Prat," Haim told her. "It flows into the River Jordan, and that's where we're going."

Denise suppressed an impulse to laugh at the name of the river.

Haim asked, "That pile of rubble over there, Denise – what do you think it is?"

"My mother would have known," she said. "She was an archaeologist."

"She'd love it here," Haim said. "Has she been on excavation teams in this country?"

"She died when I was a baby. She was only twenty-five."

"I'm sorry."

"Look over here. There's enough evidence to tell us that this was an ancient synagogue, one of the oldest in the world."

"There's building over there, behind the palm trees."

"That's a Greek Orthodox monastery. It goes back to the fifth century."

"Are there still monks there?"

"I think so. We're walking along a path that's been here for hundreds of years."

The stream widened into several still pools in the shade of palm trees. Two young men appeared, passed them and walked purposefully in the direction they had come from.

"Palestinians," Kobi said.

"They didn't look very friendly," Denise said.

She scrambled up the rocks and jumped down like a child. "This is exactly what I love to do."

They were tired and sweaty when they reached the other end of the nature reserve. A car waited for them and took them the short distance into a settlement where most of the homes were caravans.

She reached for Kobi's hand and wanted to throw her arms around his neck, but he stiffened.

At breakfast she asked Haim about training to be a tour guide.

"You'd love it. There's a lot to learn and the courses in Israel are very good. You'll have to learn Hebrew, but you'll do that in two or three years if you work hard."

Denise and Kobi were driving back to the north of the country along the Jordan Valley.

"Kobi," she asked, "what was that place we stayed at last night?"

"What do you mean?" He sounded annoyed.

"Was it a settlement?"

"Dina, you haven't been here long enough to understand."

"Are you annoyed with me?"

"Of course not. What makes you think I am?"

"You're avoiding telling me things, and I think you're angry. Like yesterday when I asked why you had guns, and now when I'm trying to find out if I stayed on a settlement."

"For fuck's sake, Dina."

When they stopped for lunch, Kobi stretched out his legs and stared at her until she felt uncomfortable. He had not shaved.

"You're so English," he said sarcastically.

"What are you accusing me for? Of course I'm English. That's where I grew up. Your dad's English too."

"My dad lives in a bubble."

"What do you mean?" she asked.

"He doesn't know what's going on in the real world." Kobi poured himself another tumbler of water, spilling some on the table. "You'll never understand the Middle East."

"I'll learn Hebrew and do a course as a tour guide. I've decided."

He laughed, or was it more of a sneer? He wiped some hummus from his lips and said, "You don't know how this country works and you never will."

He doesn't have to speak to me like this. He's annoying me on purpose.

"I don't know why you're like this today, but I don't like it."

"Calm down, Dina the Dragon."

"Do you want to tell me why you're in a ratty mood?" she asked.

"You were flirting with Haim."

"I was not."

"What made you suddenly decide you want to be a tour guide?"

"This is where I'm going to live and that's how I'm going to make my living."

"Don't fool around with me. You were flirting with Haim. Anyone could see that. You're my girlfriend. Understood?"

He in a bad mood, she thought.

"I'm sorry if I did anything to upset you. I have to think about myself, too."

"You're not serious about living here, are you?"

"My mother wanted to live here and I want to know why it was so important to her."

"I heard that she died."

"She was killed in an attack in Jerusalem."

"In the Intifada? Was it in 1987?"

Denise nodded.

"What was she doing here? It wasn't exactly the best time for tourists. There were bombs on buses."

"That's what I want to find out."

"No good asking me. I was three years old at the time."

"She spent a week on the kibbutz and your parents met her."

"I see where you get your crazy ideas from. No one but a crazy person would come to Israel as a tourist in 1987 and stay on a small kibbutz way up north."

"It wasn't so crazy. Her brother and sister-in-law lived there and they'd just had a baby. Her brother and his family went back to England. I asked my uncle and aunt about my mum's visit."

"Why are you so interested in your mum? That was more than twenty years ago. What difference does it make to you? If it had happened to me, I'd always remember my mother but I wouldn't do what you're doing."

"I haven't got any memories of her."

"Didn't you ask your dad?"

"He won't talk about her. I kept asking my grandmother and she kept changing the subject."

She had Kobi's attention, and that did not happen often.

"The story that I grew up with was that she was killed in a road accident in England. I found out that wasn't true."

"Who told you the truth?"

"No one. It was in a cutting from a newspaper that my father had hidden."

"And you found his hiding place?" Kobi thought that was funny.

"Yes. So there has to be a reason they didn't tell me the truth."

"Ask my mum and dad. They met her. But you want my advice? Ask them separately."

He pulled the car keys from his pocket. "We have to go. It's still three hours' drive from here."

THIRTY-THREE

The summer heat passed. Some days the sky was overcast, and one evening it rained. It was November. Denise was still on the kibbutz. She was living in a rented room. It had an iron bedstead with a lumpy mattress and a wardrobe with a missing door. There was a small, noisy fridge and a kettle. Her rent covered meals in the communal dining room. She filled some of her time with exercise routines and doing odd jobs with the volunteers.

A school hike in September to a park in the upper waters of the River Jordan was now a distant memory. She had volunteered to be an assistant with a group of students from the local high school.

One lunchtime, a woman wearing a windcheater, from Illinois University, asked if she could join Denise in the dining room.

"You're Dina, aren't you? My daughter talks about you all the time. You helped her so much," the woman gushed, and smiled.

"You'll have to remind me."

"The kayaks at the annual school hike? Remember now?"

"Is your daughter called Shani?" Denise asked. She nearly added, *The plump girl who ate two bars of chocolate while we were there.*

"That's her. I had to make all kinds of promises to get her to go on the hike with the rest of the class. She's overweight. She eats too much because she's unhappy and she hasn't got any friends. She's very shy and frightened of water. That's only one of the things she's frightened of; at least, it used to be. I don't know what you did for her that day but she had a wonderful time. She told me that you managed to get her to go out in a kayak."

"Good to hear she enjoyed it."

"How did you do it, Dina?"

"I pretended I didn't know a single word in Hebrew and we weren't to speak in English. We mucked around with pantomime and she thought it was funny."

"She liked you and she trusted you."

"It took a while. The rest of the class had gone white-water rafting. The leader of the hike asked me to stay with Shani. I could see she was scared. But why shouldn't she enjoy herself as well? That's what I thought."

"It worked, and now she's nagging me for swimming lessons. Would you be able to give her some? We'll pay for them, of course."

She phoned Evie that evening. "I've got work; a girl who wants swimming lessons and another two who want basketball coaching."

"And lover boy?"

"He turns up sometimes."

"Honeymoon over?"

"Real life is beginning to kick in."

"I'm coming up to Haifa to see my mom and grandma soon. I'll let you know when."

"Would love to see you."

"Someone else has a job for you, Dina," Yael phoned to tell her.

"Do you know who she is?" Denise asked.

"Her name was Ahuva or Aviva. She got my number from a friend and she wants to talk to you."

The following morning, Denise phoned the woman. "I'm Aviva, thank you for calling." The woman had an American accent and spoke in English. "I got your details from my friend and she said you're a wonderful guide."

"I'm not a guide and I don't know much about the country. But I love hiking and working with young people."

"Our organisation works with youth and you've got exactly the skills we're looking for. The kids come from English-speaking countries. They're here on programmes for up to three months."

"What would you want me to do?"

"We have leaders who have amazing depth of knowledge about the country – history, archaeology, linking the present with the past. Inspiring leaders. You'll love them. One part of the job is to accompany the groups on the *tiyulim*. The fascinating part, which you'll love, is working with the team that checks out routes and develops new *tiyulim*."

There's a catch somewhere, Denise thought. *It sounds too good to be true.*

"Could you explain a bit more, please? Which areas of the country are you talking about?"

"You're interested and that's wonderful. We go all over the country. Lots of biblical sites."

"Which parts in particular? Are you talking about the West Bank?"

"The whole of the country, Denise. The land was promised to the Jewish people in the Bible. There's no arguing with that. You're absolutely the right person for the job and you can start whenever you like. We have very good funding, so we'll be able to offer you a good retainer and when you're out with a group, you'll be paid at a good rate. Now, what do you think?"

I know what this is about, Denise realised. This was the political split that she had avoided thinking about; there were those who regarded the West Bank as land occupied by Israel and those who strongly disagreed.

That's their language, she said to herself. *They've got key phrases. 'Our land', 'the land God promised', 'our ancient homeland'. They're settlers. Peter had said that they were stealing land so that there's no hope ever for a two state solution; Independent Palestine alongside Israel.*

"Let me think about it. I've got your phone number, Aviva. I'll get back to you." She knew she would not. *If I decide to make Israel my home, I'll find out more, but right now I don't want to get into those heated arguments.*

"You'd be a wonderful addition to our team, Dina. You're an inspiration in so many ways."

Denise screwed up the paper on which she had written Aviva's phone number.

Yael wanted to know how things were working out. "We haven't seen you for days, Dina. Come round for coffee later."

Later when she was sitting on the sofa in Yael and Benjy's living room, Yael asked her whether she was finding work.

"It's beginning to happen, Yael. I'm giving swimming lessons and coaching basketball. I didn't take the job with Aviva."

She had more important things to talk about than the settlements in the West Bank. "Yael, please tell me more about my mother. What do you remember about her? What did she talk about with you?"

"I remember that she was like you. You don't look much like her, but she couldn't sit still for more than two minutes, just like you. I asked her why she rushed round all the time when she was on holiday."

"Did you believe her? Did you believe she was here for a holiday?"

"I did at the beginning. She was so happy to be with her brother. She was excited to see the new baby and she kept talking about her own baby girl, how beautiful she was and how she missed her."

Denise wriggled her toes with pleasure. "When did you start to think that she was here for something more than a holiday?"

"I asked her why she came by herself. Why not with her husband and the baby?"

"What did she say?"

"She suddenly looked unhappy. We were sitting here in this room, like we are now. I asked her why she was miserable. Was it because she missed the baby?"

"What did she say then?"

"She said she was confused. She didn't know what to do for the best. She had made a big mistake. Her husband was a good man."

"Did you ask her what mistake she had made?"

"I didn't have to. She began to talk fast, and it was difficult for me to follow what she was saying. She said she didn't know your father well enough when they married. When you were born, she told him she wanted to carry on with her work. She was still only just starting out in her profession and she was ambitious. Your father told her she could go back to work when their children left home. She told him that it wasn't just work for her. Being an archaeologist was who she was. If she couldn't learn about the past, she wouldn't feel alive. Your father told her she could read or study in her spare time. While she had small children, she would stay home and take care of them. And she told him that was not what she intended to do."

"I knew about those arguments. My father's not good at seeing other people's points of view."

"That's what she told me. She asked me whether she would be able to live on the kibbutz as a single mother with a child?"

"Was she going to divorce my father? That wouldn't have been easy."

"It never came to that, did it? But I think that's what she had in mind. I remember that she asked me whether I thought it was better to finish a marriage early or to stay with someone when you knew you'd never be happy."

"Did you give her an answer?"

"How could I?"

"Do you think she came to Israel to see if it would be possible for her to live here?"

"I'm sure of it." She paused and added, "Poor soul."

Benjy came into the house. He was still in his work clothes. Denise caught a whiff of his sweat as he passed her. "Have to shower. Join you in a minute."

"Dina, please don't think badly of your mother. If she hadn't respected your father she'd have just left him. Women do that. She was upset because she didn't want to hurt him, but she also knew she had to have a life for herself." Yael stood up. "I have to go to a meeting. You know what you should do? Ask Benjy what he thought of her. He knew her before he came to Israel. She was Peter's little sister. I'll tell him you want to talk to him."

Denise curled her feet up on the sofa and waited for Benjy. He pulled on a black pullover that had holes at the elbows and sat down heavily in the sling back chair.

"What's this about then, Dina?" He frowned. Deep furrows appeared between his eyes. *Grumpy*, she thought, and she was about to say that she'd remembered something she needed to do and had to leave. "About your mother, is it?"

She felt awkward. "Do you remember her?"

"Of course I do. I was her leader in the youth movement, her *madrich*."

"Will you tell me what you remember about her, Benjy? I can't understand why she would have left me behind and come here when it was so dangerous."

"That was typical of Gabriella. Act first and then think. She always had something to say. She was a bright

223

woman; questions about this and questions about that. If there had been one word that described her, it would be 'passionate'. She was passionate about history and archaeology. She was passionate about Zionism."

"Was she passionate about my father?"

"You get to the meat of the matter, don't you? Yael's been talking to you. That's quite a story."

Denise sensed a wave of apprehension. "Maybe I know it already?"

"I'm about the same age as Peter and your father. In Jewish circles in London, we all either knew each other or knew about each other. There weren't so many of us, after all. But I never met your father."

"Yael told me that my mother was unhappy in the marriage and that she wanted to live here on the kibbutz as a single mother."

"I know that the kibbutz wouldn't have accepted her."

He rubbed the stubble on his chin. "Can I make you another coffee, Dina? I'm making one for myself."

He stood with his back towards her. "There was Yossi…" he said.

Her heart thumped so loudly that she was sure he could hear it. "Yossi?" she whispered.

Benjy put his black coffee on the coffee table, leaned back and rubbed his hands. "Yossi was someone special. He was about the same age as Peter and me. We used to go round together. His parents are Israelis who lived in London for a few years when he was a teenager. That's how we met him. He stayed on in London to go to university. He was very bright. His parents still live here on the kibbutz."

"My mother knew him?"

"Of course. She was still at school when they met. They went round together until he got his degree, came back here and went into the army."

"And my mother was still a student?"

"That's right. So Yossi is here and she is there in London."

"I can't work this out. That was before she met my father. What year are you talking about?"

"It was 1982. That was the year of the First Lebanon War."

"Yossi was in the army then?"

"Of course. You don't want to know too much about that war. There were some tough battles."

"Did he survive?"

Benjy said, "Yes. But that war changed the way a lot of people thought about the politicians here."

"Wait. Benjy, was Yossi here on the kibbutz in 1987 when my mother visited?"

"Yes, he was."

"Was he married?"

"No, he wasn't."

"Did they get together in that week she was here?"

"Of course. You can't hide much when you live in a small community like this."

She took a deep breath, and then another. "Is he still here?"

"No."

"Where is he?"

"He went to Australia in 1989. He lives in a small town outside Melbourne. Teaches at the university and grows grapes in his spare time. He says there are fifteen Israelis living in and around the town."

"Do you think my mum wanted to get together with him again?"

"We'll never know, will we?"

"You're in touch with him?"

"We send each other New Year greetings."

"Why did he go to Australia?"

"He was totally pessimistic and disillusioned about this country. We used to argue a lot. He and Peter had similar views. They said there had to be a Palestinian state alongside the Jewish state. If settlements were built on land that should have become the Palestinian state it would get harder as the years went by to divide the land."

"Is that what you thought?"

"Me? I used to think that if the Palestinians had their own country, it would be run by terrorists. But these days I think Peter and Yossi were right. We Jews know what happens if you don't have a homeland. They want their homeland too.

"Like I say, we used to argue a lot. It was tough for me when Yossi left for Australia, and then soon after that, Peter told me that he and Margot were going back to England."

That night, Denise fantasised about the life she could have had. She would have had a happy family life on the kibbutz. The man she would have thought was her father would tell her one day when she was five or six that he wasn't her real father. She would love him so much that she would tell him it didn't matter.

She drifted off to sleep. She woke when it was still dark outside. A dream had disturbed her. An older man was telling her about his wife, and she told him that it was no business of hers. He kept telling her that his wife had left him, and she told him that she had other things to do. A white horse without a saddle stood in front of her. She leapt on its back and rode away.

The dream images of the unhappy man and the white horse stayed with her all day. She felt sad and did not know why. Anger with her mother had burned within her for years. *How could she have abandoned me?* That was a thought that never left Denise. Other thoughts cropped up. *Why did two people who were so different marry in the first place?* A photo of her mother in her wedding dress, her face glowing as she gazed at her new husband, flashed through her mind. Her father grumbled and never talked to her about her mother, but now she began to see their relationship differently. *He's a good man*, she said to herself, *even though he's prickly on the outside. He's been hurt and he tries to protect himself. If only he'd found someone kinder than Stephanie to be his second wife.*

THIRTY-FOUR

Denise was restless. *Kobi wouldn't be interested in hearing about my mother*, she thought, *but I want to tell him about the conversation with Aviva. He should have been here fifteen minutes ago.*

She tried his mobile phone again and, like the previous time, there was a recorded message. After another ten minutes, she was annoyed. She wandered over to the clubhouse and joined several volunteers who were playing table tennis. After winning two games easily, she was bored. She threw down the bat and went for a walk round the kibbutz, half expecting to meet him. *I'm fooling myself*, she thought. *Last week he said he'd be round by six and he didn't arrive until about eight. What kind of relationship is this?*

He'd phoned her early that morning, full of apologies and excuses about his motorbike and a headache. What was she doing later? He'd be round at nine.

He arrived half an hour late. She took two bottles of beer from the fridge. There were shadows under his eyes and he hadn't shaved.

"I just want to lie next to you for a while," he said, pulling her towards the bed. He asked her to hold him and stroke his hair. "This is all I need, Dina. Just hold me."

They lay still for about twenty minutes. She thought he had fallen asleep, but then he moaned and asked her again to hold him.

"What's the matter, Kobi?" she asked.

"I don't feel good," he said.

"Tell me more."

"There's nothing more to tell," he answered, and gripped her hand so tightly it hurt her.

She stroked his hair with her free hand and entwined her fingers in his curls. She'd never seen him like this before. He sat up and buried his head in his hands for a moment. Then he stood up, promised he'd be round the next evening and left.

What was that about? She asked herself as she drank a beer.

She was not sure that she wanted to see him the following evening. She did not want a repeat of his strange behaviour.

She was filing her nails when she heard him talking to someone outside the house. Who was with him? The door opened and he came in dragging one of the volunteers behind him, a Dutch girl whom Denise had never spoken to. She had long blonde hair and large breasts. She and Kobi were laughing loudly.

"Come on, Dina, try some. It's good stuff."

He pulled a small package from his pocket. He and the Dutch girl were stoned.

"I want you both to leave," she said.

"Dina, have some fun for once." Kobi laughed even louder. Holding the Dutch girl firmly with one hand, he grabbed Dina with the other. She tried to get away from him. "We've come to keep you company."

"I'm happy on my own." She had managed to wriggle out of his grip. "Get out, both of you."

He released the other girl and lunged for Denise. His arms were like steel cables. He had her pinioned on the bed.

Denise screamed. "Whatever's going on here, I don't want it. Kobi, get out now."

He was on top of her and his hand was over her mouth. She tried to kick him off, but he had trapped her.

"Calm down, Dina, nothing's going to happen that you don't want. No one's going to hurt you."

The other girl was slowly peeling off her knickers. Kobi beckoned her to come over to the bed.

"This," he began to giggle, and then to laugh convulsively, "this is what I want to do before I die. Two women and all night to enjoy ourselves."

Denise bit his hand. He let go of her and she rolled off the bed. She ran out of the house and vomited behind a large bougainvillea.

THIRTY-FIVE

"My grandmother wants to see you," Evie said. "My mom has gone to Cyprus for the weekend with her boyfriend. My grandma's got the flu and I'm looking after her. Why don't you come and keep me company? Haven't seen you in ages."

It's December. I feel like I've been living here for years, Denise thought as the bus sped towards Haifa.

"I'll bring rugs. It's cold in here, Dina."

"I love curling up on the couch and watching the lights of the city and the harbour."

They sat drinking wine.

"How's it working out?"

"It's great, Evie. I've got as much work as I want. I'm coaching a girls' soccer team next term and Weight Watchers want me to run regular exercise classes. What about you?"

"Wonderful." Evie stated, "And the fantastic man?"

"I've downgraded him. Sometimes people turn out to be different when you get to know them better."

"Is the broken heart painful?"

Denise shrugged. "I think I need to start looking for another model. It was fun while it lasted."

"You've still got feelings for him. I can see that."

"That's what I'm like. I take guys seriously."

"Hmm," said Evie sympathetically. "I know what you mean."

"Evie, what's going on? I was with Yael yesterday and she asked if I would go back home if there was a war. Is there going to be a war?"

"You don't follow the news?"

"I never listen to the radio. I can't understand Hebrew and I don't read the newspapers."

"Hamas is sending more and more rockets from Gaza. You know that Hamas has said it will never make peace."

"But Gaza is at the other end of the country."

"It's a small country, Dina."

"Do you think there'll be a war?"

"What they're saying is that Israel will retaliate against Hamas to teach it a lesson."

"I don't understand."

"It's a mosquito that keeps buzzing around. It's annoying. It won't go away. You try to swat it but you miss. So you get out all the sprays you can and a couple of sledgehammers too, and *schpritz* so that all the mosquitoes for five miles around drop dead."

"That's a war? Israel's got an army, a navy and an air force, and Hamas is a band of thugs."

"We'll drop bombs on Gaza. We've got intel and we know what they're doing. Our guys probably know exactly when and where their leaders brush their teeth in the mornings."

"Will Hamas stop sending rockets if we drop bombs?"

"You look so worried, Dina darling."

"I am worried. We don't have wars like that in England."

"You should go back home. Tomorrow."

"Kobi's a reserve soldier." Denise's heart lurched.

Evie put her arm round her shoulder.

"Evie, is he...I mean, is it possible that a soldier might be scared about fighting?"

"We all hate the wars. We have to find a way to keep going when we're always on the edge of disaster. No soldier would ever admit he was scared, even to himself. They know what's at stake."

Denise did not go back to England. Two mornings later Yael was waiting for her to get back from her early-morning run around the perimeter fence.

"Come round to our place when you finish work."

Denise was alarmed. "What's happened?"

"It's getting worse. We'll keep the radio and TV on and Benjy will translate for you."

"Has Kobi...?"

"The reserve soldiers have gone to their units."

Denise blurted, "Will he be all right?"

Yael said, "It's war. It's out of our hands, Dina."

She sat with Yael and Benjy. There was music on the radio and news bulletins broke in frequently.

"I don't know what's happening, Benjy," she said. "Do you think I should go back to England?"

A problematic relationship was not a reason to stay, she thought *but if Kobi's been strange because he's scared he might be killed, I want to be here for him. This place that feels like home, even if the others see me as English. It would be unbearable to be far away now. I could volunteer as a nursing aide.*

Denise felt frightened all the time. Her heart beat fast. Her mouth was dry. She could hardly eat. She kept waking in the night and wondering if she missed the siren. Was it her imagination, or were people rushing instead of strolling along the paths on the kibbutz? The kibbutz volunteers had all left the country.

Benjy told her that the army should smash Hamas. "They are a bunch of bloodthirsty terrorists. They've been digging tunnels under the border with Israel. They'll be planning to kidnap our soldiers, you'll see," he shouted. *Oh my God*, she thinks, *that could be Kobi.*

The television showed black smoke billowing from another building in Gaza. Yael sat bolt upright and her knuckles were white. She was silent most of the time.

"Yael is upset about the civilians in Gaza. She says we shouldn't be bombing them like that," Benjy told Denise.

"Most of them don't even support Hamas. It's not like here where we have elections," Yael said.

"They had an election and they voted for the terrorists, so they get what's coming to them." Benjy's voice was strident.

Yael explained to Denise. "Hamas uses the ordinary people as human shields. It puts its rocket launchers in crowded places. They even set them up in the hospital. But it's not right that we kill a hundred of them for each one of our soldiers."

Denise thought that Benjy was right, but she kept quiet.

"Dina, we're sending our boys in to fight another unnecessary war," Yael told her. "There are ways to settle this without all this killing."

Benjy yelled at her. "You and your bleeding heart, Yael. Our forces do everything possible to avoid civilian casualties. They send out warnings, leaflets and make phone calls."

Peter phoned most evenings. He spoke to Benjy. Denise listened and tried to follow the conversation. *Men talking military tactics*, she thought. He spoke to her and told her, "The BBC says that Israel won't let their reporters get close to the fighting. The media here in England are taking the side of the Palestinians. Phone your father, Denise, he'll be worried about you."

Time had changed. The war felt like it had gone on forever, even if the calendar announced that only two weeks had passed since the end of December. The only thing that mattered was the war. Soldiers, their faces blackened, their guns pointed, searched the ruins in Gaza. Denise struggled to identify Kobi.

THIRTY-SIX

Yael stood in the doorway of Denise's room. Denise knew that something awful had happened. Yael pulled her cardigan around her thin body. Her eyes glistened with unshed tears. She was a violin string about to snap.

"We're going to the hospital," she whispered, and her voice is hoarse. "Meet us in the car park in five minutes."

Then he's not dead, Denise thought as she threw her toilet bag and spare undies into a backpack.

The tyres screeched as Benjy sped round the bends in the main road.

"He's seriously injured and he's in the hospital in Beersheba," he told Denise.

"Did they say what happened to him?"

"Of course not."

She felt stupid for asking.

The journey was endless and silent. The roads were uncharacteristically empty of regular traffic.

In the Emergency Room, Kobi was attached to tubes and monitors. Nurses came and went. His head was bandaged and he looked as if he was sleeping peacefully.

His breathing sounded regular, and then Denise realised that a machine was ventilating him.

She stood looking at him and could not think or feel. Her legs felt weak, and then someone was helping her to walk. In the area set aside for family members of patients, she sank into a deep armchair and closed her eyes. There were people talking all around her but she did not understand what they were saying.

"They're going to operate." That was Benjy's voice. Who was sobbing quietly next to her? She reached out her hand and Yael clutched it.

Someone was holding Denise and stroking her face. She had no idea how much time had passed or if it was day or night.

"Have they done the operation?" she whispered.

It's Evie who answered her. "Yes. We have to wait and see."

"Evie, I'm no use here. I'm falling to pieces."

"Would you like to go back to England?"

She hiccupped and whispered, "Yes."

Evie patted her hand.

PART FOUR

ENGLAND

2009

THIRTY-SEVEN

Evie wheeled Denise past the rows of questioning faces in the arrivals lounge of Heathrow Airport. An older man whose tight grey curls flew out from his herringbone peaked beret rushed towards them.

"Denny, Denny. It's me. It's Daddy." He asked Evie. "What's happened to her? Doesn't she recognise me?"

"She's in shock, Graham," Evie told him. "She's gone somewhere deep inside herself. I asked for a wheelchair because she's shaky on her feet.

"Denny, it's me. Daddy is here. It's going to be all right."

Denise did not respond. Her eyes stared blankly ahead.

"We should take her straight to a hospital," he demanded.

Sweeping back her sleek hair, Evie said, "She's had enough of hospitals. You told me that you've got an apartment where I could stay and look after her for a few days."

"She's my girl, and I've never in my life seen her looking like this."

"She'll be better when she's rested. If she's like this in the morning, we'll take her to an Emergency Room."

The traffic into London from Heathrow was slow. Graham swore at other drivers but said nothing to Evie. The Rover eventually pulled into the sweeping entrance of an elegant mansion. Stone urns with clipped privets border the paved front garden.

A large window lit the marble-floored lobby where there was a black leather couch and a glass-topped coffee table with *The Financial Times*.

The flat was on the first floor.

"This is a beautiful place, Graham. Is this where you live?"

"It's comfortable and convenient. It's an investment property that I own." His voice was flat. "Four bedrooms, three bathrooms, living room, dining room and study. And a newly fitted kitchen. I've stocked the fridge. If there's anything you need, ask me. You'll stay to look after her tonight?"

"Of course."

"I've phoned my doctor and he'll be round a bit later this evening. I want her examined properly." Graham's voice was angry. "I never thought she'd be like this when she came back. I shouldn't have let her stay so long."

Graham hovered by the bedroom door as Evie helped his daughter get ready for bed. She seemed to understand what Evie asked her to do. Her face was white and her freckles stood out like small brown stains. He wandered into the living room and poured himself a whisky.

Evie joined him. "Have a look at her now. She's fallen asleep. She looks calmer."

"What's happening to her, Evie?"

"Her boyfriend is a reserve soldier and he's badly wounded. He's in hospital on life support. She stayed in the hospital for twenty-four hours. It's so tense everywhere with the war going on. It was too much for her and she couldn't cope. She asked me to help her come back here." Evie pushed her hair back. She looked into Graham's worried eyes.

Graham asked her, "What can I do to help her?"

"Let's see how she is in the morning."

When Graham came the next day, Denise, looking fragile and pale, was sitting at the kitchen table sipping soup.

"Chicken soup. I found it in the fridge," Evie said. "She's swallowed a few mouthfuls but she says it makes her feel nauseous."

Denise looked at her father. There were dark shadows under her dull eyes. "Dad," she said, "give me a hug."

It was an awkward hug. She clung to him and began to sob.

"I'm falling to bits," she said. "I don't even know how I got here? What is this place?"

He stroked her face. "This is a flat I bought, Denny. I thought you might live here when you came back. I didn't expect you'd come back like this. Don't worry. Evie and I will take care of you. You'll mend. You're a strong girl."

He turned to Evie. "I have to thank you, don't I, Evie?"

"She said she wanted to come back."

"I judged you wrong. I'm sorry."

"We've only just met, Graham. What can you know about me?"

"It was you who persuaded my daughter to stay on after she'd been in Israel two weeks. I didn't like that."

"It's what she wanted to do and I thought she was old enough to decide for herself."

"You spend a lot of time together, don't you?" Graham asked.

"We're cousins. My grandmother and hers were first cousins and were close as children."

"That hardly makes you and Denny close relatives."

Evie smiled at him. "We're still family. I haven't got a lot of relatives. She and I are about the same age and we get along."

The following day, Denise was wearing a tracksuit when Graham came.

"We went for a walk today," Evie.

"She made me," Denise.

"Have you eaten?" he asked.

"A bit."

"What would you like me to bring you?"

"Nothing, Dad. Just sit with me like you did when I was a little girl."

He visited every day. Denise hardly spoke to either Evie or her father.

"Earlier today she told me that she wants to ask you something but she's worried you'll be angry with her."

"Denny, whatever you want, my girl. Just ask."

Her voice was soft. "I want to go to Peter and Margot. I need the wind and the moor." She looked at him with tears in her eyes. "Please, Dad. Take me there."

"I'll take you, but when you get there, you have to see a doctor. You need help, Denny."

"Peter's a doctor."

THIRTY-EIGHT

Margot and Peter came out of the house to meet them and escort them inside to the kitchen, where the smell of onion soup filled the long room.

"Let's sit down and have some lunch," Margot said.

Graham hesitated.

Peter pulled out a chair. "Glad you came, Graham."

Margot stood behind Denise and stroked her hair.

"You're Frieda's granddaughter, aren't you?" Peter asked Evie. "Pleased to meet you."

Denise gasped. "It's Jade the cat!" she said. "She's on my lap and digging in her claws."

Denise showed her father her room. He picked up the photo of Gabriella and Peter as children and looked at it for a few minutes. The cat had curled up on the bed.

"Thank you for bringing me here, Dad."

He started to go downstairs, and she stayed in her room.

"Dad?" she called. He turned to her. She said, "I like it much better when you and Peter get on with each other."

Denise set a fitness routine for herself. Every day she forced herself to get out of bed and walk across the fields. Peter or Margot always went with her.

"Leave me alone. I have to be on my own. Don't you understand? I don't need to be looked after."

"It's good to see you angry again, Denby," Margot said. "A sign of recovery."

Most days, after the effort of her morning walk, she disappeared into her room, usually with the cat. Margot had to bully her into joining them for breakfast and supper.

After a week, she yelled at Evie, who was staying in Nicole's room. "I'm OK. I don't need you hanging around me any more. Why don't you go back?"

"I'll go at the end of the week. I'm worried about my mother anyway," Evie said calmly.

Denise hung her head. "Sorry I yelled. Love you, Evie."

"Love you, too."

Margot commented to Peter, "She's full of anger; the war, the boyfriend, her dream becoming a nightmare. I remember how it felt, don't you?"

"And there's something else for her to be angry about, but she doesn't know it yet. I phoned Benjy yesterday evening; he said there's no hope. Too much brain damage. They'll keep him on life support."

"That's terrible. He'll be a vegetable."

"Don't tell her. She'll have to find out in her own time."

"Sit with us for a little while, Denise." Margot invited her into the living room.

247

"No. I can't sort myself out with you guys pestering me all the time. I'm going to my room. I need my own space."

But in her room, she paced up and down, so she went downstairs again and joined her uncle and aunt, who were watching a movie on video.

"Is there anything we can do?"

"I need to get away. Be on my own for a while. And I have to be busy. I need something to do that stops me thinking. I thought of staying for a week in the Lake District and walking."

Margot asked Peter, "She could stay at the cottage. What do you think?"

Peter turned to Denise. "We bought an old cottage near Lake Coniston last year. We want to renovate it and use it for weekends away."

"Could I stay there for a few days?" Denise asked him.

"It's hardly fit for habitation. We haven't seen it since the spring. That's when we got the roof fixed."

"I don't need anything else. I'll take my sleeping bag."

"There's a wood stove that won't light, a gas cylinder and mattresses," Peter told her.

Margot added, "I'm working at home, so you could borrow my car and come back whenever you wanted."

"If I feel like doing some repairs, you wouldn't mind, would you?"

"If that's what you want to do, go ahead. We'd be delighted. There's a hardware store near the jetty and we'll pay for any materials."

THIRTY-NINE

There was a shed with some old gardening tools and a pile of firewood. It was cold and the wind whistled through cracks in the door. She lay some kindling and lit the wood stove. Within minutes, the room filled with smoke and she had to open the door and the window. She put on an extra two layers of clothing and crawled into her sleeping bag.

In the morning, a dog barking at the front door woke her. She extricated herself from her sleeping bag. Standing next to a large sheepdog was a girl of twelve or thirteen, who sniffed. She was holding a basket. "My mam said to bring you a loaf of bread and some cheese."

Denise looked at the girl, the blue sky and the cumulus clouds. She patted the dog. "That's kind of you," she said.

After breakfast, she strolled along a lane towards the lakeshore. She needed to rest when she got there, and sat on a slope looking along the length of the lake. A ferry was gliding out of the mooring, gulls screeched overhead, and a speedboat roared past and disappeared over the horizon.

Denise spent the rest of the morning sweeping and washing everything she could find. There was running water, but it was rusty brown.

In the afternoon, she drove to the hardware store in Coniston.

"You'll be staying in the cottage up the lane?" the ruddy-cheeked storekeeper asked.

"Is there anyone round here who could fix the wood stove?"

"There's a fellow staying in the village who can fix just about anything if you need him, and his prices are reasonable. I'm seeing him later. I'll send him over."

The young man came round to the back of the cottage to find Denise. She was clearing weeds in the garden. He was dark-skinned with a fine nose and short black hair. He reminded her of one of the Indian students at Exeter. He wiped his hands on his grubby, torn jeans. His sweatshirt was covered in splashed paint.

"You want me to have a look at the stove?" He spoke with a Lancashire accent.

She watched him as he methodically dismantled the stove, and she noticed that his hands were smooth with the fingers of a pianist. *He's a student*, she thought. *What's he doing here?*

"Can you fix it?"

"I'll need to replace the damper and clean the chimney flue. I'll come back tomorrow with what I need. Is that OK with you?"

He would be good-looking if he smiled instead of looking as if he's sucking a lemon, she thought.

"What's your name and would you like a coffee?" she asked him.

"Got to rush. See you tomorrow. I'm Dawud," he called over his shoulder.

Next morning, he worked quickly and obviously knew what he was doing. Denise heated water for coffee on the stovetop.

"I'm Denise. Where are you from?" she asked him.

"Rochdale," he said.

"We're almost neighbours. I live in Littleborough. Were you born in Rochdale?"

He put his head slightly on one side and raised his eyebrows. "English Pakistani. First generation. My parents migrated."

"I went to boarding school near Windermere and I spent a week in Rochdale for a school project. We were helping to paint a community centre," Denise told him.

"What did you make of the town?"

"It's another world," she said. "It's an old mill town, isn't it? The mill and the factory buildings are still there. And nearly everyone there is Pakistani. Me and my friend stayed with one of the families. They were such a sweet young couple. Some of the older women wouldn't answer when we spoke to them. That was a bit strange."

"There are still some old people who hardly speak English. They speak Urdu to their children and grandchildren."

"I remember the girl at the community centre. She was beautiful, with big dark eyes and long hair. I've forgotten her name. We painted the place together. She told us that she organised exercise and dance groups for the girls in the town."

"Was that the old church hall? The church is a mosque these days."

"That's right. Anyway, I run in the mornings, and I asked the girl if she would like to join me. She said that her brothers wouldn't let her. I thought that was weird. I've always remembered it."

"Traditional values clashing with the modern world. Happens all the time." He sipped his unsweetened black coffee.

That's something I'm very familiar with, she thought, *but I don't feel like talking about it.*

She asked, "What are you doing here in Coniston?"

"Things have been rough for me recently and I wanted to be on my own for a while to think. And you?"

"Similar story," she said.

He took his cup to the sink and started to rinse it. "Want me to look at the water?"

"Please."

He went to his van. An hour later, clear water ran from the tap.

"That's the stove and the water fixed. I'll be on my way, then."

"Wait a minute," Denise said. "I want to show you something in the garden. Whoever lived here grew their own vegetables. Would you help me tidy up the vegetable patch?"

"Waste of time and energy unless you're planning to stay for a while."

"I want to keep busy, otherwise my mind keeps

whirling round. Do you see those big stones lying around? There must have been a wall round the garden once. Have you got time to help rebuild it?"

"We can try, but the people who built these walls years ago had special skills."

"Could we work on it together for a couple of days and see how it goes?"

"I've got a couple of small jobs," he said, "but I'm free this afternoon and most of tomorrow."

Dawud and Denise collected and sorted the stones that had fallen from the wall. Rebuilding it was like doing a huge jigsaw puzzle. Dawud worked steadily, but Denise had to rest frequently. Progress was slow.

She was tired that night and fell asleep immediately, but nightmares of explosions woke her in the early hours. Was Kobi still alive? Had he known that a war was coming? Should she go back and sit at his bedside? Was the war still going on?

Next day, she felt heavy, weighed down by intrusive memories. When she and Dawid sat on the low ruins of the wall taking a break, she asked him how long he had been doing odd jobs.

"Three months," he said.

"And before that?" she asked him.

He looked at the sky and said quickly, "I had a business. Computers."

"Your own business?"

He nodded. She was impressed,

She pushed on. "Couldn't you find something better to do than fixing stoves and walls?"

He shrugged. "It's temporary work."

"Until when?"

"Until the summer." He stood up to go back to work.

"What are you doing in the summer?"

"Getting sorted out to start medical school."

"Where?"

"London."

He was looking at the sky again. "Those clouds are moving quickly. Rain's on the way."

As he left, he told her that he had to work in Keswick and didn't know when he'd finish. He'd be in touch.

Each day she felt her strength returning. She ran in spite of the rain and was nearly back to the level of fitness she wanted. After a week she'd had enough solitude, so she went back to Peter and Margot.

FORTY

Back in Littleborough, she went for runs through the Dales. The worse the weather, the longer the distance she covered.

"Feeling stronger, Denby?" her cousin Robert, home from Grenoble, asked her. "Mum said you were there when the war in Gaza broke out. What happened?"

"It was horrible and I don't want to talk about it."

"That's fine with me. Any time you want to bang on the drum, feel free. If I'm around, I'll join you and we'll blast."

"Margot, I learnt things about my mum while I was on the kibbutz," Denise said while the two of them were chopping onions.

Margot's eyes were watering. She sniffed and asked, "Did you go to the café? You said you would."

"Yes. They'd redecorated so I don't know what it would have been like when she was there. Did you know that the last person she spoke to was my dad's brother, Barry?"

"Barry? The ultra-religious guy?" Margot was surprised.

"Uh-huh. I spent Shabbat with them in Kiryat Arba. Not my scene but I'm glad I went. Uncle Barry hardly said anything to me the whole weekend. His wife's a bit of a dragon. He's like a big bear – grizzly, not the cuddly kind. I got a ride with him back to Jerusalem on the Sunday morning and asked him if my mum had seen him when she was in Israel. He said that she marched into his jewellery shop and told him that he was to remember that my father was a good man."

"Wow."

"I got the impression that he hadn't told his wife about her visit."

Margot wiped her nose with the back of her hand. "Sit down, Denise. I need to tell you about your mother."

"About why she went to Israel and left me behind when I was a baby? I think I understand that better now."

"There was more to it than that." Margot took a deep breath. "Your grandmother, Vera, used to come here and stay with us a lot. We loved having her around."

"I still miss her," Denise said.

"We all do. I learned a lot from her," Margot went on. "My mother was a depressed lapsed Catholic and my father left the family when I was a child. It was not a happy childhood. When friend of mine told me about being a kibbutz volunteer, my first thought was that I could get away from home. I knew nothing about Jews. I used to ask Vera questions, lots of questions. Some days, we would sit here in this kitchen for the whole morning and talk."

"Did she talk about my mother?"

"Whenever Gabriella's name came into the conversation, she would try to change the subject. Of course I noticed. I could see how Vera adored Peter and I thought at first it was one of those mother-daughter things. You know about sons getting more attention than daughters, don't you?

"I asked Peter about it. You know that your mother and Peter were active members of the youth movement from their early teens. They lived from one meeting to the next. Both of them had decided that they wanted to live in Israel. Your grandmother hated the idea. I said to Peter that it was natural for her to want her children to stay in England, not to leave her. He said it was deeper than that. She had very strong opinions about the country and the way it began. She told him that Israel is a country founded in sin."

"Wow. I don't see it like that at all," Denise commented.

"She tried her best to get them to change their minds. She said they had to go to university first and then they could decide if they still wanted to go. At least then they would have a profession to fall back on. Peter got a bachelor's degree and went to the kibbutz. He studied medicine when we came back from Israel. My guess is that Gabriella chose archaeology so she could work as an archaeologist in Israel. Let me wash my hands and then I'll tell you more."

They both washed the smell of onions from their hands.

Margot continued, "Peter and Gabriella were very different. Peter doesn't argue. He does whatever he's decided to do and nothing will ever stop him. He goes his own way, as you've probably noticed. Gabriella and your grandma argued about almost everything. You're like her, you know. And I think that your grandmother always knew that she would never be able to persuade Peter to do anything he didn't want to. So she tried even harder to get Gabriella to change her mind and stay in England."

"It wouldn't have helped that Gabriella fell in love with Yossi, an Israeli."

"You heard about him? He had to go back to Israel once he'd got his degree to do his army service."

"And she was still a student, wasn't she?"

"That's right. She planned to join him when she graduated. And then when Peter went to Israel, made *aliyah*, Vera did everything she could to stop Gabriella from following him."

"Is that what Oma told you?"

"She thought it was for the best. She saw that Gabriella was pining for Yossi, so she looked for a way to distract her. Your grandma was quite a manipulator. Gabriella met your father in Spain; he was on holiday and she was on a dig. He was smitten from the moment he met her. When they got back to England, he kept asking her to go out with him. Vera encouraged the match, and to this day, I don't know how she succeeded. And so Gabriella the archaeologist and Graham the estate agent married."

"And after I came along, my mother found out she'd chosen the wrong man."

FORTY-ONE

Denise looked for a detective story among the dog-eared paperbacks on the bookshelves in the living room. Peter was reading the newspaper and Margot was making lists.

Her phone buzzed. "Denise?" The voice was that of a high-pitched male or a throaty female.

"Who's this?" she asked.

"It's Felix. Don't you recognise my voice?"

"What's happened?"

"Dad's ill and Mum's off her head." Maybe he was trying not to cry. "If you kept in touch you'd know what was going on. You have to come and help."

Graham had been well when he brought her to Littleborough. How long ago was that? Not more than two weeks?

"You're there. Why don't you organise things? If he's that bad, call an ambulance."

"It's awful here. You can't imagine."

"Slow down, Felix."

"Last Friday – I always go home on Friday night – Dad was ill. Mum said he was exhausted… business troubles… needed rest." He was swallowing words.

"Go on."

"Yesterday, I phoned Mum. She said he was better. I said I'd come round after work. Mum lost it. She yelled at me: 'don't interfere, don't tell Denise' – you know what she's like. She was really weird."

"What was she saying?"

"It was... she was... trying to keep me from seeing him... She stood at the bottom of the stairs and wouldn't let me go up."

The line fell silent. She waited. She could hear him breathing fast.

"She said he'd had a lot of worries with the business. I would disturb him, she said. He had to rest and be left alone. You've got to come. Denise, are you there?"

"Yes."

"I think he's dying. You have to come. How many times do I have to tell you?"

"But why can't you sort this out, Felix? You're not a child."

"I phoned Dad on his mobile and... his voice... I couldn't hear him properly... 'Help me,' he said. 'Help me... and call Denise.'"

"Have you seen him?"

"I pushed past Mum and ran upstairs. She wasn't quick enough to stop me going into the room. Dad looked terrible... in bed... room was dark and smelly..."

"Call an ambulance, Felix. I keep telling you."

"You don't get it, do you? Mum's lost it. Even if I call an ambulance, she won't let them into the house. I've never seen her like this before. She's become a religious nutcase."

"What are you saying, Felix?"

"She's muttering all the time under her breath and carrying a prayer book around."

"Weird."

"Now do you see why I phoned you?"

"Let me think about this for five minutes."

"You have to do something, Denise... you have to..."

The line went dead.

"What's wrong?" Margot asked her. "Is it your father?"

"I have to go to London first thing tomorrow. My dad's ill and Stephanie's having some kind of breakdown. That was Felix. He can't cope with it." Her mouth was dry and her heart was beating fast.

The street was quiet. It always had been. The evening sky in March was a faint pink blush. It was cold and her fingers were numb. She pressed the doorbell of the house she had grown up in and chimes echoed inside. In the paved front garden, a standard rose bush stood pilloried at its geometrical centre. Silence from inside the house. She waited until the sudden noise of the latch being turned startled her. The door was half opened and Stephanie, looking frightened, stood there. The skin of her white face was stretched over her skull and she stared from the deep sockets of her eyes. Her black skirt hung loosely and her silk blouse had food stains on it. Her hair was uncombed.

"Why are you here?" she rapped out.

"My father is ill and I want to see him."

Stephanie tried to close the front door, but Denise stopped it with her foot.

"You aren't welcome here. Your father's sleeping and he doesn't want to see you."

Denise flushed. "That's a lie."

Stephanie tried again to shut the door. Denise pushed her out of the way. She was in the house and began to run up the stairs.

"Take your shoes off. I don't allow dirt in this house," Stephanie screamed.

Denise, who was halfway up the staircase, slipped off her shoes and threw them at her stepmother.

"He's sleeping. You'll disturb him." She followed Denise up the stairs and tried to catch hold of her legs, but Denise kicked her off. Stephanie turned and went downstairs.

"I'm calling the police," she threatened.

"Good idea," Denise shouted. "Because if you don't, I will."

She opened the door to the master bedroom, but the room, with its fitted white carpet and oyster-coloured quilted counterpane, was empty. *He'll be in the large back bedroom*, she thought. *I wonder how long they've been sleeping in separate rooms.*

There was no answer when she tapped on the back-bedroom door. The curtains were closed, and at first she could not make out details in the gloom. Graham was breathing loudly with light snores. His breath stopped at times for what seemed like almost a minute, and then he would suddenly snore. He was propped up on three or four pillows with his hands on the counterpane. The room smelled of lemon and disinfectant with an occasional unpleasant faecal whiff.

"Dad, it's me. It's Denise," she whispered.

He opened his eyes, but they did not focus on her.

"Dad," she said. "I'm here."

His voice was hoarse and almost inaudible. "Denise… you… here." He moved his left hand towards her, and now she could see that the back of it was covered in bruises. His lips were dry and there was a sore at the corner of his mouth. His breathing changed, and he tried to raise himself. He was beginning to heave as if he might be about to vomit. She found a plastic bowl and held it for him. He rested back on the pillows and she found a swab to moisten his lips. He moaned again and fell asleep. His breath smelt of acetone. A small table next to the bed was covered with bottles and packets of pills. Some saliva dribbled from his half-open mouth. The door to the en-suite bathroom was open. The rubbish bin was full of gauze, tissues and cotton wool swabs.

"Who's taking care of him, Stephanie?" she shouted from the top of the stairs.

There was no answer. She ran downstairs. Stephanie sat bolt upright on a chair in the dining room. Her lips moved. She was holding a small prayer book with the pages face down in one hand and a cleaning rag in the other.

"Who's taking care of him?" Denise said again.

Stephanie turned her head and stared at her. "As usual, you think you're in charge."

"Why didn't you let me know he was ill?"

Stephanie glared at her and spat out her words. "He is my husband. He's my responsibility. You have no right to be here. Get out."

"When did he fall ill? What happened?"

Stephanie stood up and screamed at her. "I don't know who told you to come, but this is not your house and you have no business here. It was Felix, wasn't it? The interfering, stupid boy."

"I've called an ambulance and I'm taking Dad straight to the emergency department."

Graham lay in a clean hospital bed, attached to tubes and monitors. He was dozing but responded with a nod when Denise asked him how he was feeling. He muttered something, but she could not make out what he said.

"What happened?" the slim blonde doctor asked her.

"I don't know. I'm not living in London at the moment and we're not in touch every day."

The doctor was listening.

"It may have been two weeks since I spoke to him last. He didn't say anything about not feeling well."

"We're still not sure what's wrong," the doctor told her. "He's confused and dehydrated. It's possible that he had a minor stroke." The doctor was looking at Graham's the computer. "We'll rehydrate him and then we'll do more tests."

That evening as Denise was leaving the ward, a gangly young man in a dark suit and rimless glasses came towards her. He reminded her of an untalented actor playing the part of a young accountant.

"Felix? You've changed. When did we last see each other?"

"I don't know. It's not important. I'm going to see Dad."

"I need to know what's been going on and so do the doctors."

"I don't know anything more than you. She'll be mad with me if she finds out I phoned you." Felix studied his shoes.

"Don't you understand anything? He's seriously ill. Something happened and his wife didn't get help for him."

"You're just as bossy as you've always been."

Later as she sat on an uncomfortable upright chair next to her father's bed, a hand lightly touched her shoulder. The bearded face and the homburg hat were familiar.

"It's Denise, isn't it?" The accent was guttural. "I'm Rabbi Mannheim. You probably don't remember me. I visit the Jewish patients here. May I?" He pulled over a chair and sat next to her. "How is he today?"

"He's about the same."

"Can I be of any help to you or your father?" He paused. "You've been away for some time, I believe. You came back from Israel because your father is ill?"

"No, I came back when the Gaza War broke out. He's not making progress, Rabbi."

"Patience, Denise. It is still early days."

"There is something that you might be able to help with. My brother and I think that Stephanie is having some kind of breakdown. She's acting very strangely and we're very worried about her."

He stroked his beard. "I know her mother and her sister. I'll find out."

The following evening, Graham opened his eyes and reached out for her arm. The nurses had propped him up in an armchair.

"Good girl," he said in a thick voice.

"You're looking better, Dad," she said.

"Happy... you... here." He gave her a feeble smile. He seemed exhausted. She sat with him while he dozed.

Denise sat by her father's bed in the four-bed hospital room. Intravenous fluids flowed into his arm. Graham was asleep. Small whorls of grey hair were at his throat. His eyelids fluttered.

Another doctor, a stocky woman probably in her forties, had stopped by Graham's bed and while she was looking at the computer, she asked, "You are his daughter, I imagine?"

"Yes," said Denise. "Can you explain what's happening to him?"

The doctor turned to look at Denise. "He was very dehydrated when he was admitted. And it looks like he also had a small stroke. He's making progress, as you can see."

"But is he going to be all right?" Denise asked anxiously. *The doctor looks so serious,* she thought. *What's she hiding from me?*

"It's too early to say how much of a recovery he'll make from the stroke."

"I was worried this might be the end."

The doctor shook her head. "He'll get through this. There'll be rehabilitation and we'll talk about that when we see how he's progressing." She paused and then asked, "Do you have any idea why he was so dehydrated?"

"Not really. I'm not living in London. The last time I spoke to him, about two weeks ago, he didn't say anything about feeling ill. My brother phoned me and told me that something was very wrong. I came as quickly as I could."

"Does he live alone?"

"No. He lives with his wife."

"What did she tell you?"

"We aren't on good terms and she tried to stop me seeing him."

"I see."

The doctor walked to the next bed. After she left, Denise thought of the questions she should have asked.

Graham was getting better. He could shuffle to the bathroom with a walking frame and feed himself, but his speech remained difficult to understand. He tried to talk and became red-faced with frustration. Denise was convinced he had something important to say. She was invited to meet the social worker to discuss arrangements for his rehabilitation and discharge.

The social worker, Carol, sat Denise in an armchair in her office. "I'll get straight to the point. Your father managed to convey to the speech therapist and to me that he doesn't want to go home."

"He said those words?" Denise asked in amazement.

"He understands more than he can express. He becomes agitated when we ask him about home."

"Does he say why?"

"I'm not sure that I understood his answer well enough to be able to tell you. We've also noticed that your mother has not visited."

"She's my stepmother."

"I want to ask you a bit more about the situation at home. It's just the two of them in the house these days, is it?"

Denise nodded.

"And your stepmother, dear, does she have some kind of health problem?"

"We've never got on well. I left home ten years ago."

"But your stepmother's health?"

"I saw her for the first time in a few years when I went to the house and called an ambulance for my father. It shocked me to see her. She was not in a state to look after herself, let alone my father. Something had happened to her. She always used to be concerned about her appearance but that day, her clothes were dirty and her hair was kind of wild."

"Who's taking care of her?"

"Her mother and her sister. That's what I've been told."

"And you, Denise? What are you up to at the moment?"

"Just recovering from a crisis and not quite ready for this one," she said.

"I understand. So technically you are, as they say, between jobs?"

"I suppose so."

"And where are you living?"

"In a flat in Hendon."

"I see. Would you mind if I ask you how many bedrooms there are?" Carol jotted down a note. "I'll be honest with you, Denise. We're concerned that your father was not given appropriate care after the stroke. Now I understand from what you have told me that your stepmother was unable either to care for him or to call for help."

Denise had a twisting feeling in her guts.

"Would there be an alternative once your father is ready for discharge?"

"What about a nursing home or a convalescent ward?" Denise said.

"I'm looking at possible options, but I wondered if he could stay with you for a month or two."

This was unbearable. *Don't they know that Kobi's dying?* a voice screamed in her head. Carol's voice faded. Denise's stomach ached. She would vomit. Her head reeled.

"Are you feeling all right, Denise? Would you like a coffee?"

Denise took deep breaths. "I need the toilet."

Carol was making coffee when she came back.

"Please. No coffee. A glass of cold water."

"I'm sorry. I can see that it's too much to ask. We'll see what other options there are."

Denise felt a little calmer. "What are you asking me to do exactly?"

"We know that people recover better if they're with family." Carol smiled. "I'm asking you whether your father could stay where he'll know he is being cared for. I'm not suggesting, Denise, that you give up your own life for him, but would it be possible for a few months while he is going through rehabilitation? We'll send our therapists to work with him, of course, and we'll find someone to help you. A number of our patients have done very well with this approach. It seems to motivate them to cooperate better with their therapists."

"I'm not..." Her thoughts whirled. *How can they ask me to do this? I want to feel sorry for my father but I don't. I'm selfish and I've got my own problems. What if he died while she was supposed to be looking after him?* "My stepmother will never agree to that."

"We can probably find a way to get round that."

She suddenly remembered how her cousin Evie cared for her mother.

"I'll think about it. Can we talk again tomorrow?"

FORTY-TWO

Looking after Graham in the flat was hard work. He was still unsteady, in spite of the walking frame, and Denise was constantly fearful that he would fall. At first, she could only make out a few words when he spoke. The speech therapist visited three times a week. She suggested exercises that Denise could practise with him, but he was uncooperative and she was unmotivated to push him. He was fussy about his food and she was powerless to prevent him spending hours slumped in an armchair in front of the television. Worst of all, he had nightmares and his anguished shouts made sleep impossible. She was exhausted.

Margot told her that she needed someone to be with him at night. A woman who Denise thought had probably been a prison warder took the job for a trial period. When she told Denise that her job didn't include cleaning and changing Graham after the occasional accident, Denise told her to leave. A middle-aged West Indian took her place. But after two weeks, he apologised to Denise and told her that he needed to leave because he had to look after his wife who had cancer and had taken an unexpected turn for the worse.

Denise phoned Margot in desperation. "It's fine in theory," she exploded, "but I can't find anyone reliable and Dad's still keeping me awake at night."

"I've got an idea. It may come to nothing. You remember that fellow who worked with you in the cottage in Coniston? Didn't he say he would be in London?"

"In the summer, and its only March."

"I can try to find him. I'll phone the storekeeper in Coniston, if you want."

"He's good for stoves and walls, Margot, not this kind of work."

"I thought you said he was going to medical school in the autumn?"

Dawud stood outside the door of the Hendon apartment. He was soaking wet.

"You look like you've been swimming," Denise said. "Please come in."

"It's pelting down. I can leave my shoes out here."

"Don't you have an umbrella?"

"I did but the wind blew it inside out."

He looked like a whipped greyhound with his thin, pointed face, and when he took off his raincoat, his clothes hung loosely on him. He looked around the entrance hall, with its reproduction French antique side table and gilt-framed mirror.

"Classy place," he said without a smile. "You've come up in the world since Coniston."

"My father owns this place," she murmured, and added, "I thought you weren't coming to London until the summer?"

"Plans change."

"Would you like to see round the flat or would you like a cup of tea first?"

"I'll have tea with your father." He was more relaxed than she was. "I'd like to meet him and then we can talk about the job."

She was impressed, half an hour later, with the way Dawud quietly engaged with Graham, telling him about recent football matches. She stayed in the kitchen. Graham was shuffling slowly with his frame and appeared to be showing Dawud around the flat.

Before he left, Dawud told Denise, "He's in better shape than I thought he would be from what I'd heard. Your aunt said he's been waking during the night. It will help if I sleep in his room until things improve."

After he left, Graham asked her in his halting way whether this was his new carer. "Nice fellow," he said.

Dawud slipped into their lives. He spent the nights in the armchair in Graham's room. He was so quiet that Denise hardly noticed that he was around. She heard Graham trying to talk to him from time to time but she could not hear Dawud's replies. She would hear the front door slam when he took Graham for a walk and brought him back. He insisted that he would take care of his own cooking.

Denise dozed during the daytime. She had not realised how tired she was. The nights were quieter now that Dawud slept in the room with her father. But Denise could not fall asleep. Whenever she closed her eyes she saw scenes from Gaza. Sometimes Kobi was lying in the ruins of a building. Sometimes he was kicking open a door, and she knew that the room behind was booby-trapped.

One night, unable to stay in bed, Denise padded out to the kitchen in her bare feet and found Dawud, elbows on the table, deeply engrossed in a book. She stood in the doorway for a few seconds waiting for him to notice her. He looked up when she sat down opposite him.

"Can I make you a cup of tea?" he asked, as if it was the most normal thing in the world to be interrupted by a woman in pyjamas at two in the morning.

"What are you reading?" she asked him.

"It's a book about traditional healing in India."

"I'm cold inside, Dawud. I think my insides have turned to jelly."

It was almost a minute until he said, "It's not just your father, is it?"

The kettle boiled. He had his back to her while he poured water into the mug she liked to drink from. The surge of lust was unexpected. She felt disappointed that he was wearing tracksuit pants so that his neat rear was hidden. She had to hug herself to keep from lunging at him.

"How was my father this afternoon? He said he enjoyed himself."

"I think he had a good time. He knows a lot about cricket. He knew the names of all the Australian players. Do you want to eat something?" He turned to her.

"I'd love a bowl of cornflakes. I'll get it for myself. You're here to look after my father, not me. Do you have any ideas to help me sleep, though?" She wanted to hear his voice.

She looked at him as he stood there. *His lips are a perfect, almost purple colour*, she thought. *I'd like to touch them with my fingers.*

"Warm milk instead of tea?" he suggested in his soothing voice.

"My father's doing well, isn't he?" she remarked.

"He works hard," Dawud said. "He wants to get right again."

"You have a way of getting him to work. You're better than the therapists from the hospital. They're always in a hurry. I watch you. You get him to talk." She wanted to touch him, and was impressed with her own restraint.

"It's not difficult."

"Do you think he'll ever be able to go back to running his business?"

"Maybe."

"Will you stay until he's better?" she asked.

"I'm here to take care of your father while he needs help. As you said, Denise, he's getting better."

You've made it completely clear that you're not here for me at all and I hate you for that, she thought.

"Do you want more cornflakes, or maybe a piece of toast?" he asked.

"I wish you'd stop acting as if you're a servant here."

She saw that he wanted to get back to his book but he was too polite. She knew she should go back to bed and leave him alone, but she couldn't get her legs to move. Anyway, this game eased her pain.

"Kiss me, Dawud," she invited him, moving her face slightly towards his.

"No, Denise."

A red monster growled inside her head, and a voice that she didn't recognise spat out, "Don't you like women?"

"You should go back to bed, Denise." His tone was measured.

"Maybe you should join me?" she said in an exaggerated seductive tone.

"I'm going to sit with your father. Goodnight."

She went back to bed and punched the pillow.

The next day while Dawud and Graham were out, she searched Dawud's belongings. She had to know more about him. She usually respected other people's privacy, but that was not important. In a side pocket of his backpack she found an envelope with two photos of an attractive young woman with long dark hair, shining eyes and a smile that says she loved the photographer.

"What happened in Rochdale? Something happened. What was it?" she demanded when she came into the kitchen around midnight. The night was cool and she was wearing slippers and a dark blue dressing gown. "I looked in your pack. Who's that woman in the photos?"

He remained impassive. "Denise, I think it's best for both of us if I leave as soon as possible and you find a replacement."

He mustn't go, she thought. She put her hand on his arm.

"You're so cold to me. You only see my father. Can't you see what a state I'm in?"

"Of course I see. Please don't take offence, Denise, but what you ask me to do is not part of my work and I can't stay under these conditions."

"What a prick you are. You're a man and I'm a woman. We're trapped in this flat. It's not real life, it's a horror movie."

"You employed me to look after your father. We have to keep this arrangement strictly on a work level." His fists were clenched and he was speaking through his teeth.

She dug her nails into his arm. "I hear you. I'm screaming for help. I must know who that woman is. Is she your wife?"

"It has nothing to do with you, Denise." He was icy.

The smiling woman in the photos taunted her. Denise exploded. "Tell me. Tell me."

"You'll wake your father."

He turned away from her. She grabbed the book he was reading and held it behind her back.

"Give that to me, Denise," he hissed.

"I'll throw it out the window if you don't tell me who she is."

She held the book in her raised hand and he gripped her wrist until it hurts. She welcomed the pain. He pulled the book from her hand.

"Please tell me."

"She was my cousin. She's dead." He buried his face in his hands.

"I'm sorry, I'm so sorry. I wanted to hurt you. I didn't know."

"I'm going to bed. You should too."

In the morning she was calmer. Dawud was getting her father ready to go out for their walk. She caught his arm to stop him leaving.

"Could we talk for a while, please?"

Dawud took off Graham's overcoat and sat him down opposite the TV. "We'll go out later. It's going to rain," he told him.

They went into the kitchen.

"Please forgive me. I don't know what happened to your cousin, but I know how awful it is when someone you love... and you hurt so much inside, and it doesn't make sense, and you wonder why it had to happen, over and over again." She was crying.

"What happened, Denise?" He sat next to her, but did not touch her.

"I was in Israel for a few months. I met this guy. I suppose I was too serious about him. I hadn't felt like that about anyone else. It was like my whole life changed. I don't believe in these things but it felt like destiny. I was sure we'd get married and I'd live in Israel for the rest of my life."

Dawud listened intently. She went on, "I was so happy that I didn't take much notice of what was going on. People were beginning to talk about another war. Kobi, that was his name, acted a bit strange. I was completely into what I thought was my new life and I didn't think about what he might be going through, being a reserve soldier and knowing he'd be fighting."

She paused.

"Then the war in Gaza started and everything was different. The radio and the TV were on all the time but I don't speak Hebrew so I couldn't follow what was happening. I hated the way the terrorists kept sending rockets into Israel. They were attacking my country, that's what I felt. People told me to go back to England but I didn't want to leave. I wanted to help. It sounds stupid. I thought I could volunteer to help in a hospital.

"I sat with Kobi's parents and watched terrible scenes on the TV. I kept looking at all the soldiers in their helmets and blackened faces to see if I could recognise him."

Dawud nodded. Her voice became louder.

"Then his parents and I rushed to the hospital. He was wounded...badly...a head injury. We waited at the hospital while they operated. I know he won't recover. Half his brain is on that blood-soaked ground. Then, suddenly I couldn't bear it any more. He wasn't dead and wasn't alive. It won't change until someone turns off the switch. The dream of my new life disappeared like water down the plughole."

"I'm sorry, Denise." He touches her hand and says nothing.

"I've always thought of myself as a strong person. If there's a challenge, I'll find a way to meet it. It was like I had slammed into a brick wall. All I wanted was to come back home...and I didn't have any idea of where home was.

"Is there something I can do to help, Denise?"

"I want to phone Kobi's father. Will you sit with me while I do that?"

The phone rang for a long time before Benjy answered. He spoke mechanically. "He's still in the hospital in Beersheba."

Denise asked "Is he conscious?"

"No. They did another operation yesterday. They said it was to relieve the pressure. Dina, it's not good."

"What did they say?" she asked.

"There's been a lot of damage. At least he's alive at the moment. He's not in pain. We have to hope."

Denise turned to Dawud and buried her head in his shoulder.

That night, she came into the kitchen where he was staring at the book in front of him, and she knew he wasn't reading. He was waiting for her. He would not look at her. His skin was grey. He whispered, "They murdered her, Denise. My cousins and my uncle. They murdered her. Family honour, that's what they said."

"Oh God, that's terrible."

"She was full of ideas. You'd have liked her."

Denise had a flashback to her trip to Rochdale when she was at school; the church hall that she helped paint. *Was she the young woman in the pink tracksuit?*

He went on. "Terrible, Denise; senseless barbarity, like your war in Gaza." He stands up. "I'm going to check on your father."

Her knees were trembling. She went back to bed and falls asleep almost immediately.

She was woken by Dawud, who was gently shaking her.

"You were screaming and groaning," he said. "We shouldn't have talked."

The next night was windy and stormy. Denise tossed and turned for at least an hour. It was after one in the morning when she went into the kitchen for a glass of water. Dawud rubbed his eyes and closed his book.

"Does it ever heal, Dawud?"

"I don't know. I keep hoping it will, because it's unbearable."

"Yes," she said.

"Your father keeps me busy during the day and I forget about it for a while."

"I don't want to forget my lovely dream. I need to hang on to the memories of good times."

Dawud nodded.

They sat in silence. Graham's snores could be heard from the bedroom.

"Will I ever sleep normally again?"

"No point in asking me, is there?"

"I have to ask you something," she said. "What did you call it – your cousin's murder?"

"Senseless barbarity," he says.

"A good description," she says. "All that killing. Children, women, bombs, fear, rockets. Do you understand why it has to happen?"

"It's the way a lot of people see the world. Their family, their tribe – that's who they are."

"I don't understand how your uncle and your cousins could have murdered her."

"It's about the family and the tribe. In their eyes, she had dishonoured her family and her people."

"Would you tell me about her?"

"She fell in love with a man who wasn't a Muslim."

"But did she have to be killed for that? My uncle married a non-Jewish woman."

"Do you really want me to tell you about my family?"

"Neither of us can sleep and yes, I want to know."

"My uncle and my father are brothers. When they came to England from Pakistan, they had totally different ways of dealing with living here."

She yawned, but she was not bored.

"You're tired. Go back to bed. We'll talk about it another time," he said.

"I'm not tired," she protested. "As soon as I get into bed I'm wide awake."

"My father said to himself, *We live here in England so we'll make this our home. We'll learn what England is about and how to become brown Englishmen.* But my uncle is different. He said to himself, *I'm going to make myself very rich in this cold, miserable country that exploited my people for hundreds of years.*"

Denise nodded. "I know the type."

"Then along came the next generation. My uncle and aunt have three children, two boys and then a girl. My parents are not so lucky. They only have me."

"I'm beginning to like you, Dawud. They weren't unlucky."

"Thank you for the compliment, Denise, but you don't know me. Anyway, that's not the point. My cousins, Ali and Suleiman, grew up in Rochdale like I did. They were smart at school. They were spoilt, rich brats.

"Their sister, Jamila, was just as smart as her brothers at school. But she was a girl. Her parents and her brothers told her how she was going to live her life and she didn't like that. She didn't fight with them. She came round to our house so often that we were like brother and sister. My father argued with his brother about Jamila's future. You understand?"

"Yes, Dawud, and I like the way you explain it."

"About two years ago, Ali, he's the older brother, started going to the mosque all the time. Suleiman followed him. There are imams who are influencing young men to become more radical. Ali grew a beard, just round the edge of his chin, and started to wear a kaftan.

"My father talked to my uncle. He said what was being taught at the mosque was dangerous. My uncle kept saying, 'It's good that they're more religious.' They had arguments that turned into screaming matches. In the end, my uncle and my father stopped speaking to each other."

Denise remembered her weekend in Kiryat Arba. "We have religious fanatics in our family, too. My father's brother is one of them."

"So you know what I'm talking about. Ali and Suleiman began to make life miserable for their sister. They told her how to dress, who to talk to, where she could go. She couldn't go out without a chaperone. They wanted her to stop going to college, and were planning to marry her off to someone they chose. She wouldn't listen to them. She spent even more time at our house. Jamila is – was – a bit like you, Denise. She was determined to live her life as she wanted to. She used to go for runs until her brothers stopped her. They told her that no decent Muslim woman wears a tracksuit and runs on the trails outside the town."

Denise remembered how the young woman refused the invitation to run with her when she was in Rochdale.

Maybe she was Jamila, but she doesn't tell Dawud that. There isn't much point.

"Then Jamila met this guy. He's Welsh and not a Muslim. She wouldn't tell me his name or how they met. I think she was protecting him and me. She swore me to secrecy and told me that they were planning to elope."

"This is so sad," Denise comments.

"My parents and I were invited to a family party at my uncle's house. We were surprised because my uncle and my father had stopped speaking to each other. They said that they had arranged a marriage for Jamila. She was going back to Pakistan to marry a wealthy widower. The party was very festive, with too much food. But the odd thing was that Jamila wasn't there, so I asked where she was. My aunt said she was running a fever and was asleep upstairs. I said I wanted to see her. They didn't want me to, but I crept upstairs anyway. She was asleep, but thinking about it afterwards, I'm sure she was drugged. It didn't make sense. I knew it wasn't right and I keep blaming myself for not smuggling her out of the house that night."

"Wouldn't that have been impossible?"

"It might have been difficult but I didn't even try. Anyway, the next morning they'd all disappeared. A neighbour said that a removal van came in the early hours. A month after that, the police found her body. She'd been strangled." He spoke in a whisper. "I'm sorry, Denise. I shouldn't have told you."

"It's strange. Somehow hearing about your loss and your pain makes me feel a bit less alone. It doesn't take the pain away, though."

"Perhaps your soldier will recover."

She thought for a while. "It doesn't sound like it."

"The war in Gaza; the TV producers know that violence brings them viewers. It's almost like pornography. Sitting in your armchair and watching people being killed in front of you, live on TV. You keep watching until the horror doesn't even register. We're all being desensitised to brutality," Dawud says.

"You don't talk like a handyman from the Lake District."

"I fixed your stove, didn't I?"

"Don't forget the stone wall."

"I'm good at those things."

"Are you a Muslim, Dawud?"

"Yes, but I'm not observant."

Denise was aware that she felt calmer than she had for days, and the kitchen felt safer.

"I'm tired. Maybe I'll manage to fall asleep."

The next afternoon, while Graham was resting, they talked again in the kitchen.

"Do you understand why I had to get away from Rochdale?" he asked her.

"Yes, completely."

"Will you go back to Israel?"

"I might. At the moment I'm not sure what I want to do."

"But you came back to England?"

"I can't explain it."

"Did it help, being in the Lake District?"

"It was a relief to be in a place where I knew what was going on."

"What's it like in Israel?"

"Bits of everything. Desert, hills, the sea, noisy people, modern and busy, and then a bit further along the road you're looking at hasn't changed for centuries."

"Your face lights up when you talk about it."

"Does it?"

"But you're English, aren't you?" he asks.

"So are you."

"If someone asks, I tell them I'm English and my parents came here from Pakistan."

"I was born here to English parents. Being Jewish makes it complicated for me. I'm not religious at all. How can anyone believe in a loving God who allows the things we've talked about to happen? Being in Israel made sense to me, and being in England makes sense too. Do you know what I mean?"

"People don't fit neatly into boxes, Denise."

She thought about what he said. "That is absolutely true. You think you know about someone and then you find out that they're not like that at all."

"Like your soldier?"

"I saw everything, including him, through rose-tinted glasses. When I think about it now. I realise that he may have been scared of being injured or killed and that the country's got problems."

"Why did you go there?"

"My mother died when I was a baby. She was killed in a café by a terrorist bomb when she visited Israel."

"Did you find out why she went?"

"Yes. I found out a lot of things about her that I didn't know before."

Dawud looked thoughtful. "I don't know much about Israel except that there's amazing medical research at the Weizmann Institute," he said.

"I'd like to show you round one day."

"It might not be for a few years."

"Doesn't matter. I get the feeling that we'll stay in touch."

He gave her a strange stare, and there's another long silence.

"Would you marry a non-Jew, Denise?" He looked serious.

"Is that a proposal?"

"No. I would never propose to a woman in her kitchen. Especially if there are dirty cups in the sink."

They both laughed.

"Are you married, Dawud?"

He hesitated. "I was for a short while. My mother arranged a marriage for me. She's more traditional than my father. I didn't argue with her. I thought that it might work out. I was twenty-two and she was nineteen."

"How long did it last?"

"After the first few weeks, it was clear to both of us that we didn't like each other and probably never would."

"You sound so casual."

"It may sound odd but it wasn't important to me. I let my mother make the decision. Sounds stupid, doesn't it? As far as I know my ex-wife remarried, and I think she has a child."

"Why did you ask me if I would ever marry a non-Jew?"

"I wondered if you feel you're part of the tribe and that it's forbidden to marry outside it. I was thinking about Jamila. She was ready to marry outside the tribe and she paid for it with her life. It's such primitive thinking."

She paused. "I know that when I fell in love with Kobi, it felt like I was becoming more like my real self. Do you understand?"

"I think so."

They didn't talk, and it didn't matter. Then Dawud broke the silence. "It's the middle of the night. It's probably not the best time to have a serious discussion about the problems of the Middle East with an English Muslim?"

She smiled at him. "I'm not tired."

He made tea for both of them and sat down again. He looked serious. "We think of ourselves as belonging to our tribe. We're comfortable with those we think of as our own people. We know their customs and their history. But we have to learn to live outside our own little boxes. Do you understand what I'm trying to say?"

"Yes, and I think you're right. My cousin Evie taught me that. She has an Arab boyfriend."

Dawud was thinking deeply again. "Denise, I think you should visit. Those relatives and friends that were important to you when you were there, they'll want to see you. And you need to see your soldier again, even if it's to part from him."

She wanted to tell him to mind his own business, but he was right.

FORTY-THREE

Kobi lay as if sleeping peacefully in the hospital bed. Regular breathing huffed from a machine and another mechanical device devoted to his continued survival hummed in the background. Fluid flowed in and out of his damaged body. His head was bandaged, his eyes closed. Lines flowed across screens. Nurses, doctors and other members of the hospital staff wearing surgical gowns came and went, checking monitors and dressings.

Yael sat upright and unmoving on a chair. Her eyes were blank, her cheeks sunken, and her hands lay loose in her lap. Denise pecked her dry cheek. Benjy slumped on another chair, sighed deeply and reached out his hand towards her. Evie and some of the soldiers from Kobi's unit were in a room set aside for family members. She joined the vigil at Kobi's bedside. No one spoke.

There was food and drink, but there was no day or night. The world outside melted away. Denise stared at Kobi's pale, almost unrecognisable face, wanting to touch him. The soft rhythms of the machines and her numbness almost hypnotised her.

On the fourth day, she gently kissed Kobi's cheek.

Thank you, Kobi, for love and fun. I have to go now. I didn't understand. I'll always love you, she said in her heart.

She squeezed Yael's dry hand, hugged Benjy and Evie, and then turned and walked away.

On the flight back to London, the person sitting next to her was a dark-skinned older man; maybe an Indian Jew, she thought. He smiled at her. "First time I've been there. Wonderful country. One of my sons lives in Ashdod. Should have gone years ago, but it was never the right time. Were you on holiday?"

"Not exactly," she replied. She hoped the man didn't want to talk.

"They've achieved so much. Excuse me." He swallowed a pill and closed his eyes. "Have a good flight."

They sat in the living room, Graham in his leather reclining armchair and Denise on the sofa. Dawud was cooking a 'welcome home' meal for Denise in the kitchen.

"Smells good," she said.

The living room and its ceiling moulding were softly lit by floor lamps.

"Pleased you're back, Denny." Graham beamed at her. "How was it?"

"It was awful, Dad. My boyfriend was badly injured."

"I know. But the hospitals there are the best in the world. How's he doing?"

"Not well."

"Is he going to recover?"

When she didn't answer, he asked, "Did he speak to you?"

"He lies there and it looks as if he's asleep. He's connected to a breathing machine." Her voice was flat.

"My poor girl." He shook his head. "Terrible."

She needed to change the subject. "How have you and Dawud been getting along while I've been away?"

"We're managing well. My speech gets better all the time. I went into the office for the first time yesterday morning."

"That's good."

"We all have to find a way to go on when these things happen. I'm beginning to put my life together, Denny. And I want to tell you something. You and that Indian fellow have taken care of me in an amazing way." He spoke more slowly than before the stroke and some words were still slurred.

"His parents are from Pakistan, and he was born here, Dad."

"Bright fellow. He's going to medical school. He'll make a good doctor."

"I see you got him to do the cooking while I was away. I left stuff in the freezer for you."

"He asked me about the Jewish dietary laws, so I taught him. Every dish he cooks is kosher. By the way, I told him to go easy on the chilli tonight. I don't want to wake up in the middle of the night with a furnace in my belly."

He wiped some saliva from the side of his mouth. *My poor father*, she thought, *what did you do to deserve what happened to you? And Kobi, who drove too fast and made me laugh? Why do these things have to happen?*

A wave of misery swept over her. Graham heaved himself out of the armchair and came to sit next to her. She rested her head on his shoulder and he patted her back with his good arm.

"My dear old dad," she sniffed.

Dawud announced from the kitchen that he would start bringing in the dishes in fifteen minutes. Graham moved back to his armchair and Denise asked him, "When do you think you'll go back home, Dad?"

"Not quite ready yet."

She nodded.

"Tell me the truth, Denny – when I was in the hospital, did you think I was going to make it?"

"I wasn't sure for a while."

"I don't remember much about those first few days. I tried to phone you and I dropped the phone. And then you were there." He smiled his slightly lopsided smile. "I thought I was dreaming."

"Felix phoned me."

"And you came, Denny. That meant everything to me."

"Of course I came. You're my father."

"When you went off to Israel, I thought I'd never see you again."

"It's a five-hour flight, that's all."

"My head told me that you'd be safe, but I couldn't stop thinking about your mother."

"I knew you were worried, Dad, but I couldn't let that stop me."

He chuckled. "I tried, didn't I?" He swallowed a

mouthful of orange juice and gazed wistfully into the nearly empty tumbler. "When you were growing up, I felt that you hated me at times."

"You always took Stephanie's side. You didn't know what it was like for me."

"Stephanie needed protection from you. You could be awful." He patted her shoulder again and said. "I never understood how a little girl of three or four could upset a grown woman so easily."

She grinned. "It wasn't difficult. She would tell me what I had to do, how to put my toys away, what shoes to wear, how to eat my food. Whatever she told me, I'd do the opposite."

"She meant well. She wanted us to be a family."

"She tried to push my oma out of my life. Her ideas and mine about what makes a family weren't the same. Are you in touch with her?"

"Not directly. It's for the best. I know what's happening. She's better than she was. But she can't manage on her own. They're not sure if she ever will."

"Who's taking care of her?"

"She's in a private nursing home. Felix visits every week. He says she's well looked after and seems calmer." He straightened himself in the armchair.

"And you, Dad – when are you thinking of going back to the house?"

"You asked me that a few minutes ago. I'm still thinking about it. What about you, Denny? What are your plans? Do you think you'll go back to Israel?"

"It turned out to be different from what I planned. I didn't expect the sense of belonging that I felt when I was there. My mother probably felt like that, too. Do you understand? It's where I feel at home and I'm sure I'll go back one day. Right now, though, I don't have plans."

"Your mother's visit turned out to be different from what she expected too." A wave of sadness spread over his face. She nodded.

"So, Denny, where are you off to next?"

"Scotland for a week. There's a rock-climbing course I want to do. It'll be good for my career as a tour guide, and I'll enjoy myself."

"And after that?"

"Not sure whether India first and then Australia, or the other way round. Don't look so worried, Dad. I'm not going until you're settled."

Dawud brought in the meal. He set dishes on the dining-room table and explained each one.

"Denny, I have to tell you about this fellow," Graham said. "Did you know that he's a Muslim?"

Dawud passed round the dishes and the chutneys. *I wish he wouldn't act like a waiter*, Denise thought.

"It's a vegetarian meal." Graham commented. "Says he gets the spices from a store near Golders Green Station. Try the onion bhaji, Denny, it's excellent."

"Dawud," she commanded, "sit down and eat. You're one of the family. *My* family." Then she asked him, "Have you found a place to live when you start medical school in October? You'll be a mature student. You won't want to be in digs with those crazy young school-leavers."

"I'll manage," he said.

Graham pushed away his dinner plate and said in a loud voice, "I've got an idea. A very good idea, even if I say so myself."

Denise and Dawud looked at him.

"I want to go back to my house. But I won't be able to manage on my own."

"Why go back to the house, Dad? You own this flat. You could live here."

"That house is my home. I've lived there for more than twenty years." He paused. "What would you say, Dawud, if I asked you to move in with me as my carer with light duties?" He went on without giving Dawud time to reply. "I trust you and I like you. Now, young man, you're going to need a place to live when you're a student. You'll get free board, and wages, of course. Think it over. As far as I can see, it'll be good for both of us."

Denise added, "And for me, too. I'll know someone's keeping an eye on you, Dad."

"He's not just *someone*, Denny. He's a very special fellow. In fact, if he was Jewish he'd make you a good husband."

"I wasn't planning on getting married for a while." She smiled at both of them, stretched across the table and squeezed their hands.